THE GRAVEYARD
OF THE PACIFIC

THE GRAVEYARD
OF THE PACIFIC

Shipwreck Tales from the Depths of History

ANTHONY DALTON

VICTORIA · VANCOUVER · CALGARY

Heritage House Publishing Company Ltd.
www.heritagehouse.ca

Library and Archives Canada Cataloguing in Publication
Dalton, Anthony, 1940–
    The graveyard of the Pacific: shipwreck tales from the depths of history / Anthony Dalton.

Includes bibliographical references.

ISBN 978-1-926613-31-4

    1. Shipwrecks—British Columbia—Vancouver Island. 2. Shipwrecks—British Columbia—Pacific Coast. 3. Ships—British Columbia—History. 4. British Columbia—History. I. Title. II. Title: Shipwreck tales from the depths of history.

FC3844.7.S5D35 2010   971.1'2   C2009-907010-3

Series editor: Lesley Reynolds.
Cover design: Chyla Cardinal. Interior design: Frances Hunter.
Cover photo: *Tuscan Prince*, aground on Village Island in Barkley Sound. Courtesy of the Maritime Museum of BC.
Proofreader: Karla Decker

Mixed Sources
Cert no. SW-COC-001271
© 1996 FSC

The interior of this book was printed on 100% post-consumer recycled paper, processed chlorine free and printed with vegetable-based inks.

Heritage House acknowledges the financial support for its publishing program from the Government of Canada through the Canada Book Fund (CBF), Canada Council for the Arts and the province of British Columbia through the British Columbia Arts Council and the Book Publishing Tax Credit.

BRITISH COLUMBIA ARTS COUNCIL
Supported by the Province of British Columbia

Canada Council for the Arts   Conseil des Arts du Canada

13 12 11 10   1 2 3 4 5
Printed in Canada

For all those who challenge the sea

Contents

Prologue

CAPTAIN OSCAR MARCUS JOHNSON *stood perfectly still, staring out from the bridge at the foredeck. No more than 100 feet in front of him, but hidden in the fog, a lookout stamped his feet and rubbed his hands to ward off the cold and damp. Although in the bow, he too could see nothing but grey ahead. Johnson looked at his fob watch. It was 9 o'clock. He called for a sounding. "No bottom, sir," the answer came back.*

"Bring her round to north one half east," Johnson ordered the helmsman.

Outside, the fog shrouded the ship. Valencia turned onto the new heading, sailing blind. Captain Johnson believed they were somewhere off Umatilla Reef, Washington. At 9:30 p.m., he called for another sounding. "80 fathoms, sir," came the

reply. Half an hour later, a new sounding showed 60 fathoms.
"Come round to north three-quarters west."

Another sounding at 10:30 p.m. gave a reading of between 56 and 60 fathoms. At 10:45, the lead showed 80 fathoms; 15 minutes later, the depth was again 60 fathoms. The reading was down to 40 fathoms at 11:15 p.m., and 20 minutes later it showed 30 fathoms. Captain Johnson squinted into the gloom ahead. "Where are we?" he asked himself silently. None of the soundings made sense based on where the ship should have been. Close by, Second Mate Peterson flicked his gaze from the captain to the fogbound deck in front of them.

As the leadsman reported 30 fathoms, Captain Johnson brusquely ordered, "West 35 degrees north." Valencia began her turn, carving an invisible white wake behind her. At 11:45 p.m., the soundings showed only 24 fathoms.

The minutes passed. The tension on the bridge could be felt by all three men. Peterson willed his eyes to see through the murk. The lookout in the bow huddled his head deeper into the collar of his rain gear. He pulled the brim of his hat down over his eyes, which were stinging from the cold. Without knowing it, he fell asleep on his feet.

Less than 15 minutes after the last sounding, Peterson saw the colour of the fog change. A black mass reared up directly in front of the ship. Captain Johnson saw it at the same time. As one, they yelled at the helmsman, "Hard a starboard."

Valencia's bow veered round to the west, but it was too late. The ship plowed into the rocks.

Introduction

ON COLD, WINDY, WINTRY NIGHTS, when rain and snow bring visibility down to almost zero over the seas off the southwestern coast of Vancouver Island, one can almost hear the moans and groans and screechings of dying ships. Mixed with the unearthly sounds of tortured wood and metal are the low, mournful wailings of the ghosts of the long-dead passengers and crews who died on or close to the rocky shores. They were mostly men, but among them were a handful of women and a few children.

Most were within hours of the end of their voyages. Some were coming from California, others from far-distant foreign ports. A few were just setting out on their voyages. Without exception, none of them expected to be shipwrecked in the Graveyard of the Pacific. None of them were prepared to die so close to their destinations or their points of departure. Of the few who made it to shore, many died of exposure before they could be rescued.

It was because of these ill-fated ships and people, and for all those who would follow, that the now-famous West Coast Trail was originally developed. Between 1888 and 1890, the government strung a telegraph line through dense bush on the west coast of Vancouver Island, using traditional Native trails and linking villages and a couple of towns with the recently built lighthouses at Cape Beale and Carmanah Point.

Following the *Valencia* tragedy of January 1906, when far more than 100 people lost their lives, public opinion persuaded the government to do more in case of another equally deadly shipwreck. As a result, the Pachena Point lighthouse was built and a few life-saving stations were established. The barely visible telegraph trail was also greatly improved and marked so that shipwrecked mariners could find their way to safety.

Much later, the installation of radar on ships and the invention of other greatly improved navigational devices significantly reduced the number of shipping disasters on the coast until the life-saving trail was no longer considered necessary. It was abandoned and allowed to deteriorate. In 1973, the old trail became part of the brand new Pacific Rim National Park and was upgraded. Hikers now enjoy the trek along coastal trails where the ghosts of long-dead mariners may still roam.

1

The Earliest Wrecks in the Graveyard

SAILING SHIPS HAVE BEEN PROBING into Juan de Fuca Strait since at least the final decade of the 16th century. As far as we know, the first Europeans to reach this region were Spaniards, followed by the British. For them there were no lighthouses, no foghorns and no navigational charts of the coastal waters. There were no accurate maps of the coasts and the myriad islands that we now know make up this vast and complicated region.

When the first Spanish explorers arrived, they had to navigate with extreme care, never knowing what was beyond the next fog bank. When Captain James Cook sailed into these waters in early 1778, there was no one to warn him of an exposed reef at low tide. There were no weather reports. Like all the early mariners, he felt his way along the coast with extreme caution and admirable skill. We will never know how many perished in the unpredictable winter storms. We do know, however, that many of those early explorers passed on to later mariners the knowledge that this Pacific Northwest, despite being incredibly beautiful, required exceptional seamanship. There was another potential problem for survival: the indigenous people were not always friendly, and some were known to attack and set fire to foreign ships.

Captain Cook missed Juan de Fuca Strait on his voyage up the west coast en route to the Arctic. He landed in Nootka Sound, about 100 miles northwest. Perhaps he and his two ships, *Resolution* and *Discovery*, were lucky in managing to avoid that particular hazard.

Noted British Columbia underwater archaeologist and historian Fred Rogers claims that 26 sailing ships were lost on this coast in the decade between 1850 and 1860. Most of those were victims of inclement weather and uncharted currents. Modern charts show the wrecks of at least 20 vessels on the coast of Vancouver Island between Port San Juan and the east side of Nitinat Inlet. As the distance in a straight line is less than 20 miles, that means there are the remains of one ship for every mile of coastline. The greatest concentration is clustered around Bonilla Point, Carmanah Point and the entrance to Nitinat Inlet. Looking farther along the coast, there are places where the concentration of wrecks is much greater.

Captain Edmund Fanning's action-filled sketch of J.J. Astor's ship
Tonquin under attack by Natives in Clayoquot Sound in 1811.
CAPTAIN EDMUND FANNING

Between Port San Juan and Victoria, on the Canadian
side of the strait, there are about 50 wreck sites. Most of those
are close to Race Rocks or just outside Victoria Harbour. In
the opposite direction, there are another 25 wrecks in the 20
miles from Nitinat Inlet to Barkley Sound. Continuing up
the coast all the way to Cape Scott, there are about another
100, though scattered more widely.

Only 33 years after Captain James Cook visited
Vancouver Island, an American fur-trading ship owned by
John Jacob Astor of New York arrived in Clayoquot Sound.
Tonquin was a three-masted barque of 290 tons. She was 96
feet long and, unusual for a merchantman, equipped with

10 guns. When the white-hulled ship dropped anchor in Clayoquot, the Native people were apparently ready and willing to trade. Unfortunately, *Tonquin's* Captain Thorn, an arrogant man known to have a violent temper, insulted the Native chief Nuukmiis, by ordering him off the ship when they could not agree on a price for otter pelts. Thorn added to the insult by striking Nuukmiis in the face with a pelt.

The Native villagers, members of the Tla-o-qui-aht, were incensed. A few days later they paddled out in canoes, apparently to resume trading. Once on board the ship, they produced weapons from their bundles of furs and attacked to avenge the insult to their chief. In the ensuing fight, they killed all but five of the ship's crew. Four were later captured and tortured to death, but one, a man named James Lewis, enticed the warriors back on board, ignited the powder magazine and blew up the ship, himself included. No one knows how many died that night, but one story told of body parts floating all over the bay with the wreckage. Tla-o-qui-aht women and children had gone out in the canoes with their men. Waiting alongside, they too perished when the ship blew up. *Tonquin* was not strictly a victim of the Graveyard of the Pacific, but her explosive ending is the stuff of legend on the Vancouver Island coast.

At the western end of Juan de Fuca Strait, where so many wrecks rest, the unlit coasts of Vancouver Island on one side and Washington on the other waited for unwary ships coming in from the Pacific Ocean. Even in the strait they were not safe; navigation, in winter weather particularly, was always a hit-or-miss affair. Ships that made it through the strait safely still had to successfully pass the spread of Race Rocks en route to Victoria or Vancouver. Washed by a tide race that runs up to eight knots, Race Rocks stand one nautical mile from the southernmost point of Vancouver Island. Up to late 1860, before the completion of the Race Rocks lighthouse, the cluster of weather- and wave-worn granite projections just west of the entrance to Victoria Harbour was a nightmare for shipping. Only three days before the lighthouse went into operation, a 385-ton British square-rigger, *Nanette*, carrying an extremely valuable cargo for the Hudson's Bay Company plus machinery for a sawmill, passed Cape Flattery light and entered the strait. Then, after a 175-day voyage from England, the trouble began.

Thick fog blanketed Juan de Fuca Strait when *Nanette* sailed in under the command of the first officer. Manoeuvring carefully under shortened sail, with just enough canvas up to maintain momentum and steering control, she was caught by the tide and pulled in toward the coast. Crew members took soundings, swinging the lead often and with precision. Others stood by the anchors, ready to let them go at the first command. The fog drifted in and out.

Race Rocks came in sight in mid-evening during a short break in the fog. The mate wrote in the log, "At 8 o'clock saw a light bearing N by W. Could not find the light marked on

Race Rocks is a natural hazard washed by swirling currents about 10 miles from Victoria off the south coast of Vancouver Island. The lighthouse was built between 1859 and 1860. ROYAL BC MUSEUM, BC ARCHIVES B04180

the chart. At 8 1/2 o'clock it cleared somewhat, and then saw the point of Race Rocks the first time, but no light. Called all hands on deck, as we found the ship was in a counter current, and drifting at a rate of 7 knots toward the shore. We made all possible sail, but to no avail." The light they had seen, but not found on their chart, was almost certainly the Fisgard light, installed in 1860 to mark the entrance to Esquimalt Harbour.

Caught in the grip of the current, *Nanette* rode up onto the rocks during the night, and there she stopped. She flooded quickly, but the crew were able to get off at first light.

The wreck being so close to Victoria, looters soon arrived in small boats and interfered with official salvage operations. A large force of police had to intervene, and some of the looters were arrested. One report told of six men in overloaded canoes who drowned while making for shore. A few weeks later, *Nanette* slid off the rocks in a gale and sunk. Her scattered remains were never salvaged.

Even after the lighthouse came into operation, Race Rocks and other obstructions nearby continued to lure ships ashore. On November 6, 1877, Bedford Rock, just two miles west of Race Rocks, was the scene of another sinking when the 735-ton, iron-built British ship *Swordfish* ran aground in the early hours of the morning in calm conditions. *Swordfish* was in ballast, coming from San Francisco and planning to pick up a cargo of lumber bound for Australia from Vancouver's Hastings Mill. Caught in a current and turned around, she hit hard, stern first. The captain tried to sail her off, but to no avail; within 15 minutes, the hull was half-full of water. He sent distress signals, but no one came to help. The crew were in no immediate danger, so the order to abandon ship was delayed until it was light enough to see the land. Then, at daybreak, the captain ordered the crew to take to the boats with whatever valuables they could carry. He and a few others stayed near *Swordfish*, watching with despair as the waves broke her and it became obvious she would never sail again.

Race Rocks, aided by the currents, acted like a magnet for ships. They claimed the SS *Rosedale* on December 12, 1882, followed by another freighter, *Barnard Castle*, on November 21, 1886. *Barnard Castle*, under Captain Urquhart, had departed Nanaimo carrying 2,300 tons of coal for San Francisco. Having been on duty all night, the captain briefly handed over command to the first officer at 5:00 a.m. He gave one last order before he left the bridge deck: "Call me when we are off Race Rocks."

A few minutes before 6:45 a.m., or thereabouts, the first officer called Urquhart. As it happened, he was too late. *Barnard Castle* was already in the current and about to strike. She hit the outer part of the reef with considerable force before the two officers could react and turn her. She glanced off, however, instead of running her bow up and becoming trapped. Captain Urquhart made the sensible decision to run her into Esquimalt. Before he could do so, she was found to be badly wounded and filling with water. Engine-room personnel shouted that the fires under her steam boilers were about to be extinguished by the flood. Urquhart turned for the shallower waters of Pilot Bay on Bentinck Island and beached her there on the mud.

Captain Urquhart's decision to beach her was the correct one for the cargo and crew, but not so for the ship. *Barnard Castle* never moved again. The cargo of coal was taken off, but the ship remained with her keel embedded in the glutinous mud of the bay, while storm after storm tore her apart over the next few years.

Another ship carrying coal for San Francisco failed to

San Pedro was carrying coal from Comox to San Francisco when she came to grief on Brotchie Ledge near Victoria in 1891.
ROYAL BC MUSEUM, BC ARCHIVES A-00137

get past the natural hazards off Victoria in 1891. *San Pedro*, an iron steamship of 3,119 tons, was loaded with 4,000 tons of coal at Comox and sailed on November 28. She was guided by experienced officers. Both her captain and a licensed pilot were on the bridge. The pilot, Captain James Christensen Sr., was on board to take the ship through the Gulf Islands and was scheduled to be dropped off outside Victoria Harbour. They passed safely through the dozens of islands that make up British Columbia's Gulf Islands and Washington's San Juan Islands. With the lights of Victoria blazing on shore to starboard, *San Pedro* passed Trial Island at 8:00 p.m. and reduced speed to dead slow ahead.

The shallowest part of Brotchie Ledge is only submerged by nine feet at low tide. In 1874, its position was marked by a bell buoy, but no light. The buoy was visible in daylight and would have been audible with any wave action. The night that *San Pedro* slowed to drop her pilot was dead calm. The buoy sat upright over the submerged reef without making a sound. Although the two officers and lookouts searched for the buoy, they did not see it.

At 8:30 p.m., *San Pedro* struck the ledge and came off, only to hit again much harder. This time she stayed put, caught by the bow. The tide was falling, and *San Pedro* was in a desperate position. Captain Hewitt, the ship's commander, ordered full steam astern, but his ship refused to move. He immediately sounded distress signals with the steam whistle as *San Pedro* listed dangerously with her stern low in the water.

Two tugs answered the call for help. *Standard* and *Wellington* came alongside at 11:00 p.m. and began to take off coal to lighten the ship. No one knew then that *San Pedro* had suffered a 30-foot-long gash in her hull below the waterline. When the tide was at its lowest level, she hung off the ledge at 45 degrees. The next high tide failed to lift her; instead, while men were on board taking off her cargo, she moved suddenly, causing a rush to get off. The panicked workers threw themselves into the sea and swam for their lives as *San Pedro* slid off the ledge and went down. The swimmers all got to safety, most being picked up by other boats. *San Pedro* settled on the bottom, with only her wheelhouse and part of the foredeck above water.

Over a period of time, the rest of the coal was taken off. *San Pedro*, though, could never be salvaged. A storm sent her into deeper water, and there she remained for a few years, an untidy-looking wreck, eminently visible at low tide and in sight of a city.

2

A Mystery Wreck

NOT ALL SHIPS THAT MET their end in the Graveyard of the Pacific did so on forbidding coastlines. A few were wrecked out at sea. Most of those incidents were well recorded, except for the final fatal moments when a ship went down with all hands. Occasionally a mystery would play out as an unknown hulk was found adrift on the seas off Vancouver Island or the Washington coast.

One such vessel was reported in January 1874 when the crew of a British naval barque named *Prince of Charles* saw an upturned hull drifting with the northbound current off the Washington coast near the Oregon border. There were no signs of life and no possibility of taking her in tow, so the *Prince of Charles* sailed on to her destination, where her captain duly reported the sighting of the unidentified ship.

Two months later, on March 22, a wreck was seen off Cape Flattery by another ship. This wreck too was floating bottom and keel up. The American steam sailer *California* moved in for a close look and estimated that the wreck was about 300 tons and reasonably new. They passed that little snippet of information, plus her location at the time they saw her, to the authorities in Victoria. A floating wreck is an extreme hazard for other ships, and the one thing not needed in the Graveyard of the Pacific at any time was another hazard.

Grappler steamed out from Esquimalt soon after, under the command of Captain Rudlin, to salvage the derelict if it could still be found. An upturned hull, no matter how large, would not be easy to find in rolling swells or breaking waves. With his knowledge of the waters of Juan de Fuca Strait and the Pacific Ocean side, Rudlin soon found the hull, and his crew managed to get a line on it. Looking down, they could see through the water that the mystery ship still had its two masts in place and all sails set. The obvious conclusion from that evidence was that she had turned over, without sustaining too much damage, while under way in a normal fashion. *Grappler* struggled with its prize for six hours without gaining more than a few hundred yards toward any port. By this time her coal was running low, and she had no choice but to release the tow and return to Esquimalt.

The next day, she went out again with her bunkers full, accompanied by HMS *Boxer*. As soon as they reached the scene, both ships' crews managed to get lines aboard the hull, and slowly, working together, they took it in tow. It was hard going in heavy seas. Over the next eight hours, the two ships battled to keep the wreck moving in the right direction, breaking a few towing lines in the process. After each breakage, their crews had to again take huge risks to re-establish connection. Finally, after dragging the wreck no more than four miles, they were forced to admit defeat. HMS *Boxer* tried to sink the derelict with three well-aimed shells, but she stayed afloat, now a few miles out from Cape Flattery.

Both ships returned to Esquimalt to refuel. *Grappler* went back to her regular business. A day later, HMS *Boxer* steamed out again to find the wreck. With *Grappler* busy, she was escorted by a sidewheel steam tug, *Isabella*. It took those two powerful ships the best part of 48 hours to find, take in tow and haul the wreck back to port, where they anchored her, still inverted, well in toward the beach.

By this time, the upside-down wreck was known to be a 360-ton schooner named *Elida*, which had sailed from Coos Bay, Oregon, sometime the previous year with a crew of 18 men. She was loaded with lumber and coal and hadn't been heard from since she sailed.

When *Elida* reached Esquimalt, a navy diver examined the wreck and confirmed that the masts and sails were still intact. Attempts were made to right her by running cables around her hull to pull her back up, but without success. It's probable that the drag of her masts and sails, still underwater, had much to do with that. Then the owners arrived and sent another diver down to inspect *Elida*. He disputed the previous diver's assertion about the masts, stating that they were gone. All that was left hanging, he said, were the anchors from their chains in the bow. He also said there were three bodies floating in a cabin.

It's possible, of course, that the masts snapped off while the ship was in shallow water, sometime after the first diver's inspection and perhaps even during the righting attempt. In that case, they could have floated away between the two underwater surveys. Although subsequent efforts were made to roll her upright, *Elida* refused to cooperate. Another diver explored her, but he found no trace of any bodies in the wreck. There is no record of what became of *Elida*'s remains. It's probable that she was towed away from the land and sunk in deep water.

3

Three Ill-Fated Sailing Ships

PRIOR TO THE INSTALLATION OF lighthouses or other warning beacons along the southwestern coast of Vancouver Island in the mid- to late-19th century, the region—as we have seen—was a notorious death trap for shipping. Wild storms, thick fogs, heavy rain or snow and difficult currents conspired to lure even the most skilled of mariners to disaster. Even so, the advent of flashing coastal lights and powerful foghorns did not altogether eliminate the threat of grounding on the rocky shore.

At the end of December 1852, a lighthouse commenced operations on Tatoosh Island, off Cape Flattery, Washington. High on land and with a powerful beam, in good weather it was visible for 20 miles out at sea. Its location marked the southern entrance to Juan de Fuca Strait, gateway to Victoria, Vancouver and Puget Sound ports. In 1872, a steam-driven foghorn was added to the light as an extra warning to mariners. The Cape Flattery light, as it became known, was without doubt the most important navigation aid at the time to ships' officers installed on the Pacific side of either the Washington or British Columbia coasts.

Despite Cape Flattery's bright light, the local fog and notoriously inclement weather, combined with an unpredictable and potentially deadly northbound ocean current, caused the waters immediately outside Juan de Fuca Strait to continue to claim more than their share of ships, especially in winter. In the three years between 1884 and 1887, three barques, or sailing ships, came to grief.

The first was the 434-ton American ship *Lizzie Marshall*. She sailed out of San Francisco Bay for an unspecified British Columbia port on February 7, 1884. Two weeks later, she was off Cape Flattery when the wind died and fog descended on the land and ghosted onto the sea. For some reason, the foghorn was not in operation that day; enveloped in thick fog, Captain Adolph Bergman had no way of knowing his true location. *Lizzie Marshall* drifted with the current, rolling from wave to trough, her spread of canvas hanging loose and wet, unable to sail out of its relentless grip without a wind.

Carried north by big Pacific Ocean swells, the square-rigger soon fetched up off Bonilla Point, on Vancouver

Island, almost due north of Cape Flattery. Seeing disaster ahead, Captain Bergman had the crew drop two anchors in 20 fathoms of water in a desperate bid to hold his ship off the lee shore. He then sent a lifeboat manned by four volunteers to row across the 15-mile-wide strait to Neah Bay. Their orders were to find a tug to haul *Lizzie Marshall* clear of danger.

The rowing team made it after a hard few hours, but the weather had already turned against the ship. A southwest gale blew in, quickly clearing the fog. At first, *Lizzie Marshall* held her position, but by the morning of February 22, she was in more trouble as her anchors began to drag. To lessen her profile to the wind, the crew cut away the masts and all rigging and dumped them alongside. It was not enough. The wind blew stronger, and the anchor chains, already under enormous tension, parted. With nothing to hold her back, the ship swung around and plunged broadside onto a reef, with the stern jammed between rocks. In spite of the heavy surf, the officers and crew were able to scramble ashore. One man, a German sailor, drowned when he foolishly went back on board to collect his clothes.

Before long, local Natives arrived by sea and scavenged the wreck. In doing so, their own boat was shattered on the rocks, leaving them stranded as well. Eventually a tug did arrive from Neah Bay and took off the ship's personnel and the Natives.

Less than two years later, on November 20, 1886, another American sailing ship, *Charles B. Kinney*, set sail from

An artist's rendition of Cape Flattery lighthouse on Tatoosh Island, Washington. NOAA. COLLECTION OF ELINOR DEWIRE, SENTINEL PUBLICATIONS

Port Townsend with a full load of lumber for Australia. Once beyond Tatoosh Island and out of sight of land, she disappeared with all hands. Almost one month later, a battered hulk drifted ashore near Cape Beale and was seen by the local lighthouse keeper. Before any attempt could be made to positively identify her or check for people on board, she sank, leaving only her masts showing. The only suggestion he saw of a name was "Charles B." A piece of wreckage found later on the beach also bore the name "Charles."

About the same time that *Charles B. Kinney* went missing, the steam tug *Hope* found a large sailing ship, almost submerged but still drifting, just off the coast a couple of miles east of Cape Beale. The only identification that could be made was the letters "C" and "E." It has never been ascertained whether or not it was the same ship or if either wreck was the missing *Charles B. Kinney*. The only known facts are that the barque *Charles B. Kinney* never did arrive in Australia and no member of her crew was ever seen again after she departed from Port Townsend.

The huge *Duchess of Argyle* was a fast British four-masted barque of 1,700 tons (almost four times the size of *Lizzie Marshall*), built of iron in 1874 at Stockton-on-Tees, England. She was 253 feet long with a beam of 41 feet. She carried four tall masts, and her iron hull was further strengthened with double decks and watertight bulkheads.

The *Duchess* sailed in ballast from San Francisco on October 13, 1887, bound for Vancouver, where she was to take on a load of lumber for Melbourne, Australia. Her skipper, Captain H.E. Heard, said the first two days were calm with light winds. The weather changed abruptly on October 16, when a "fierce gale" struck the square-rigger and blew for 10 full days and nights. By the time the winds died down, Cape Flattery was visible from the masthead, about 20 miles away to the northeast.

The following morning, as the *Duchess* wallowed in unpleasant waves off the Washington coast, the tug *Pioneer* came alongside, presumably to assist the big ship through Juan de Fuca Strait. Captain Heard later reported the events

The lighthouse at Tatoosh Island with Cape Flattery and the entrance to Juan de Fuca Strait seen in the right centre.

NOAA. VK947.D4 1869

as they had unfolded: "We got the hawser aboard, lowered the upper topsail and clewed the top foresail up, and were just clewing the main and mizzen lower topsails when the tug signalled the ship to slip the hawser."

The reason given for the sudden release was that the heavy seas caused the stationary sailing ship to roll too much for the safety of the tug. The smaller vessel just could not keep her under control. At that time, Cape Flattery was only 14 miles away, but often obscured by fog banks.

The captain takes up the story again: "At midnight a strong gale came up from the eastward and the weather cleared. The ship dropped Flattery light bearing east by south. The gale lasted only a few hours and [then] the fog returned again. On November 1 at 4 p.m. the fog lifted and Cape Flattery bore southeast by south a distance of three miles." The fog obviously came back thicker than ever; for the next two days, "the weather was so thick" that they could not see either shore or the strait.

On the afternoon of November 3, at 3:15, lookouts and other crew on deck heard the sound of surf crashing on shore. The captain reported, "First Officer W. Spurr was in charge of the ship . . . with visibility down to a cable's length of the bow . . . Orders were then given to put the helm hard down, but she refused to answer and continued to make for her place of destruction. A few moments later the bow struck a rock, upon which the yards were backed and she came off. Another swell then threw her hard on the reef, where she came on broadside and started to pound. The bottom soon stove in and the hold filled with water."

There was nothing more the captain or crew could do. Captain Heard gave the order to abandon ship, and the men lowered boats on the leeward side and moved aboard. The captain, as custom demanded, was last to leave his ship, at 5:15 p.m., and the boats made their way carefully along the coast looking for somewhere safe to attempt a landing. They went ashore for the night at Port San Juan, seven miles to the northwest, and returned to the wreck in the morning. By then, the doomed *Duchess* had sunk at the bow up to the second deck at low tide, although the stern was quite high out of the water. The crew salvaged some clothing before being taken off by another ship, which had seen the distress signal (an inverted Union Jack) flying from the masthead.

Just over a week later, Captain Heard returned with a marine inspector to what was left of his ship and found she had sunk in a gale. Reports later showed there had been little left on her when she went down. In the absence of the crew, Natives had come aboard and looted her of anything of value.

4

The *Pacific* Disaster of 1874

SIDEWHEEL STEAMERS JUST DON'T HAVE the streamlined appeal of smooth-hulled vessels. They don't look right in heavy seas either, where their big wheels seem fragile and out of place. Despite that, sidewheelers were used regularly along both coasts of the United States in the 1800s, as well as in European waters. On the Pacific side of North America, the Cassiar gold rush of northern British Columbia, which started in 1873, created a huge need for ships to carry men and supplies from California to Victoria and Vancouver. At that time of great urgency, almost anything afloat—or close to it—would do.

While the gold fever mounted, a 24-year-old wooden sidewheeler lay rotting from neglect on the mud flats of

San Francisco Bay, where many aged vessels spent their last years in the 1800s. Being on the mud was nothing new for the *Pacific*, which had sunk in the Columbia River in July 1861 after hitting a rock. She was recovered on that occasion and continued in service until 1872, when she was beached. She would probably have stayed on the mud flats if Bahamian miner Henry McDame hadn't found gold up in the Cassiar. Once word of McDame's find reached Victoria and spread far and wide from there, the rush was on. As a result, *Pacific* was purchased by a San Francisco company in 1874 and supposedly renovated—at great expense, the owners claimed—for a quick return to the sea.

Pacific sailed north for Victoria on October 26, 1875, and had an uneventful voyage. After unloading and making a side trip to ports in Puget Sound to pick up cargo and a few passengers, she again called in at Victoria. There she took on more cargo and a lot more passengers. By the time she was ready to sail, she carried in excess of 2,000 sacks of oats, an unknown quantity of sacks of potatoes, 300 bales of hops, 18 casks of tallow, 6 horses and 2 dogs, a couple of buggies, 261 animal hides and 2 cases containing opium. There were 11 casks of furs, 31 barrels of cranberries, 10 cords of wood bolts, 280 tons of coal, a few tons of general merchandise and a strongbox said to contain $79,200 in cash.

Also on board, in addition to the crew of 50, were well over 200 passengers and their luggage—exactly how many is not known, because some reckless late arrivals jumped aboard without tickets as the ship left the wharf. One report said the ship's decks were "so crowded that the crew could scarcely move about the decks in the discharge of their duties." Estimates put the number of people aboard at 275 or more. Many of those passengers, having just come down from the Cassiar to avoid the imminent winter, would have been carrying considerable amounts of gold with them.

The sidewheeler waddled away from Victoria Harbour at 9:30 a.m. on November 4, 1875, half an hour later than scheduled. Her master, Captain Jefferson D. Howell, a handsome and popular native of Mississippi, was on the bridge when she left port. Captain Howell had nine years of experience on the west coast and was no stranger to the treacherous ways of its northwest currents and storms. He should have known that the ship's safety depended to a great extent on her stability. Unfortunately, he neglected that aspect of his duty. Consequently, *Pacific* was not a pretty sight as she left the harbour. Instead of sitting proudly with her decks horizontal and her masts vertical, she heeled to starboard. The hurried loading had resulted in uneven weight distribution. To keep the vessel in trim, the crew moved sacks of potatoes from one side of the ship to the other and asked passengers on deck to move across as well. Out in Juan de Fuca Strait, the crew kept the ship in balance by filling the lifeboats on the high side with water. When the ship heeled the opposite way, they opened the bungs and let the water flow out, while they then filled the lifeboats on the opposite side. It was, at best, an unusual and desperate attempt to maintain stability.

Pacific was a lightweight for her size. She was 225 feet long and 30 feet wide but only registered at 876 tons, which suggested she was not strongly built. Later, a simple analysis of parts of her hull would show that her timbers were also rotten. It was said that the wood "could be pulled apart by a person's fingers."

As *Pacific*'s paddlewheels thrashed the waters that morning, pulling her toward the Pacific Ocean, another ship was heading in from the opposite direction. *Orpheus* was a sturdily built and well-maintained wooden square-rigged sailing ship of 1,100 tons. She was inbound for Nanaimo, on the east coast of Vancouver Island, to pick up a load of coal.

Pacific passed Cape Flattery light at 4:00 p.m. Her course was south-southwest into a fresh southerly wind, which slowed her down a little. Rain was falling as darkness fell, and whitecaps littered the heavy ocean swells. The only lights to be seen were the running lights on port and starboard, the masthead light and possibly a few cabin and saloon lights. Everything else was black. The sails, which would have lit the ship to some extent had they been full, were furled against the yards. The sounds were those of a labouring ship and the ever-moving sea. By this time, Captain Howell had left the bridge. Neil Henley, a young quartermaster, had the helm, and the second officer was in charge.

At 8:00 p.m., the watch changed. Another quartermaster took over the helm, and the third officer took temporary command of the bridge.

Meanwhile, Captain Sawyer sailed *Orpheus* along the Washington coast, close enough to shore to see Cape Flattery's light when they reached that latitude. That beacon signals the south side of the entrance to Juan de Fuca Strait. If he missed it, the current would soon set him on the rocks of Vancouver Island. Surprisingly, considering Cape Flattery had not been sighted, Sawyer left the bridge at 9:30 p.m. after handing over to Second Officer James Allen. Neither of them knew it, but they were still about 40 miles south of the cape and 12 miles out from land.

From his cabin close to the bridge, Sawyer heard Allen shout an order to the helmsman to turn hard to port. That took the wind out of the big ship's sails, and she slowed almost to a halt, slewed at near right angles to her original course. Sawyer returned to the bridge and asked Allen what he was doing. Allen replied that there was a light off the port bow and that it was Flattery light. Sawyer knew that Allen was wrong and said so. Unless the ship was going south instead of north, the lighthouse would be to starboard. Then he saw a light on the starboard side. Another ship was coming straight at *Orpheus*. The second officer's order had taken her across the bow of the oncoming *Pacific*.

While the crew swung the yards to catch the wind in the sails and get the square-rigger moving out of the way,

Sawyer watched the lights, expecting the oncoming ship to alter course to avoid a collision. But the lights got bigger until the sidewheeler's bow rammed into *Orpheus* forward of her starboard beam. A lesser vessel might have been mortally wounded, but the square-rigger was tough. The impact rocked *Orpheus* and swung both ships around until they hit again side-on a couple of times before passing each other by.

At a later inquiry, Captain Sawyer claimed he hailed *Pacific* immediately following the collision and asked her to stand by, but received no reply. A crew member on the square-rigger reported water coming in below, but that proved false. *Orpheus* had suffered damage, but it was not life-threatening. She had taken a heavy couple of hits along one side, with planks stove in, and some rigging and a 40-foot length of rail had been carried away. The captain's first responsibility was to his own ship, but the laws of the sea required that in the event of a collision, both ships were to make sure the other was safe. *Orpheus*, the crew discovered, had not been holed below the waterline and was in no danger of sinking. Captain Sawyer could have stayed at the scene to determine the damage to the other ship, yet he continued on his way. In doing so, he inadvertently condemned 277 people to death. It was not until the next day that anyone noticed part of the *Pacific*'s bow tangled in the rigging.

Aboard the crippled *Pacific* there was chaos. The ship was listing far to port, and water was rushing in from the open bow. Passengers and crew milled around in confusion.

The sidewheel steamer *Pacific* was lost off Cape Flattery, Washington, in 1875 when she collided with the sailing ship *Orpheus*.
LEWIS & DRYDEN'S MARINE HISTORY OF THE PACIFIC NORTHWEST, PORTLAND, 1895

There had been no lifeboat drill on departure for the passengers and no orders given to the crew detailing their stations. No one, it seemed, knew how to launch the lifeboats. One lifeboat filled with passengers before it was ready to be swung out over the side, making it impossible to launch.

Lifeboats were launched as the ship settled deeper into the sea, but they were overcrowded and handled by unskilled passengers and crew and soon overturned in the rough seas. The funnel broke loose and fell overboard. *Pacific* was bow down and listing badly when she broke in two. Both sections sank almost immediately. Only 20 minutes had passed since the collision.

Cast into the sea, most of the women drowned when their long skirts soaked up water and dragged them under. The few survivors clung to any piece of wreckage big enough to support them. One large piece, part of the hurricane deck, carried eight people, including the captain and one woman. As the night wore on and the weather deteriorated, waves regularly broke over the makeshift raft. At about 4:00 a.m., a breaker swept away the captain, another officer, the woman and another man, leaving only four. A few hours later, soon after daybreak, another man died and rolled away. Now only three men clung to the raft, praying for a rescue ship. Other pieces of wreckage held a few more people, two here, one there, but not many. At the end of that long day on the hurricane-deck raft, another man died. Sometime during the night, he was followed to eternity by one more. Now only one man survived—the ship's 21-year-old quartermaster, Neil Henley.

Some distance away, separated by breaking waves and unknown to Henley, passenger Henry Jelly lay spread-eagled on the remnants of the pilothouse. He was a 22-year-old Irish civil engineer, and he was still very much alive. A ship passed in the night, but no one on board saw the wreckage or heard the cries of the few survivors still clinging to life. Thirty-six hours after the sinking, lookouts on a northbound ship, *Messenger,* saw a man adrift on a raft. Henry Jelly had hung on to life long enough to be saved. *Messenger*'s captain sent his boats to scour the area for other survivors, but none were found. Somehow they missed Neil Henley. When *Messenger* arrived at Port Townsend with the news of the disaster, the US revenue cutter *Oliver Wolcott* was dispatched to the scene to conduct a search. The crew of that vessel found Neil Henley four days after the sinking. He had drifted to the mouth of the strait and was the only other survivor to be found. *Oliver Wolcott*, with Henley on board, continued its patrol.

Over the next few days and weeks, bodies were picked up by other ships. Some drifted with the currents and were found well inside Juan de Fuca Strait; one was discovered tangled in weeds close to Victoria, about 100 miles away from the sinking. Most, however, were never seen again.

But what of *Orpheus*? Although only superficially damaged, her time was running out too. Her officers never did see the light from Cape Flattery, and they missed Juan de Fuca Strait. On November 5, Second Officer James Allen saw a light to starboard, which he assumed was Cape Flattery. It wasn't. Since the ship's last visit to the Pacific Northwest, a new lighthouse had been built at Cape Beale on Vancouver Island's southwestern coast. Allen saw the light, assumed it was Cape Flattery, and made his turn to starboard, thinking he was entering Juan de Fuca Strait. Instead he drove his ship up on the rocks of Tzartus Island in Barkley Sound. It was perhaps fitting that Captain Sawyer and his crew, all of whom survived the wreck, were picked up six days later by *Oliver Wolcott*, the same ship that had rescued Neil Henley.

The subsequent inquiries into the disaster, held in Victoria and San Francisco, could have proved that *Pacific* was unsound and far from seaworthy, but a whitewash by shipping inspectors effectively avoided that outcome. No charges were laid at the company's doors, and due to lack of concrete evidence, no proof of guilt could be held against Captain Sawyer for sailing away from the wreck. The *Pacific*'s owners, Goodall, Nelson and Perkins, restructured the company two years later into the Pacific Coast Steamship Company, which also would experience serious problems on the high seas, especially in the Pacific Northwest.

The tragic collision between *Pacific* and *Orpheus* 135 years ago still ranks as the worst maritime disaster on the west coast of the United States, but it was a disaster that could easily have been avoided. If one believes in the fickleness of fate, it's interesting to note that had *Pacific* left Victoria on time, and had the southerly wind not slowed her passage down the Washington coast, the two ships would almost certainly never have met in that vast open ocean.

5

Janet Cowan
Meets Her End

WHAT LITTLE REMAINS OF THE four-masted, steel-hulled barque *Janet Cowan* lies on the seabed approximately 12 miles south of the north end of the West Coast Trail. The few scattered relics have been there since early 1896, after she ran aground on the southwestern coast of Vancouver Island on New Year's Eve.

The weather was atrocious that last day of 1895, as it had been for two weeks or more. Gales blowing at up to 50 miles per hour from the south and west played havoc with shipping. The winds brought a mix of rain and sleet, which reduced visibility to a minimum. None of this was particularly unusual for the season or for the region, but for a sailing ship trying to find her way into Juan de Fuca Strait from the Pacific Ocean, and with a strong north-flowing current, it was a recipe for disaster.

Janet Cowan was built of iron on the Clyde at Glasgow, Scotland, in 1889 by Barkley, Curly & Co. She was 308 feet long with a beam of 44 feet. She was listed as being 2,578 gross register tons and she could carry almost her own weight in cargo. Owned by R. Shankland & Company's Burn Line, *Janet Cowan* made only six long voyages in six and a half years. During that time, she knew two masters. On her maiden voyage, Captain MacKay took her from Penarth, Wales, to Montevideo, Uruguay, and Calcutta, India, returning to Dundee, Scotland, 13 months and 3 days later. That initial voyage established a pattern for the ship for the next few years. Her second voyage, also to India, kept her and the crew away from home for 11 months and 25 days. On his third voyage in *Janet Cowan*, Captain MacKay was ordered to take her first to Cape Town, South Africa, then on to Calcutta and back to Hull, England. Considering her size and build and that she was sail-powered only, *Janet Cowan*'s passages showed quite respectable times, such as 119 days from Calcutta to Hull via South Africa's Cape of Good Hope.

After her third voyage, Captain Magnus Thompson, a 48-year-old Shetlander, took command. *Janet Cowan* was taken off the India run and sent to South Africa at the end of November 1892, loaded with coal from the deep Welsh mines. Captain Thompson's first voyage on his new ship lasted 15 months and one day. It took him from Hull to Falmouth and Barry (both British ports), then to Table Bay, off Cape Town. From there, the ship ran east to Newcastle, New South Wales, Australia, taking 50 days for the voyage. Just under three weeks later, she set sail for San Francisco, her first visit to North America, spending another 78 days at sea. Loaded with grain, *Janet Cowan* slipped her moorings in the beautiful bay in late October 1893 and spent the next 152 days—her longest passage—sailing back to Hull to complete a circumnavigation of the globe.

After another fast run down the Atlantic to South Africa, she left Cape Town on her ill-fated final voyage with 1,000 tons of ballast in her holds (probably rocks) on September 11, 1895. On board, in addition to the captain, were 28 sailors. Lightly laden and sitting high out of the water, *Janet Cowan* sailed east with the current across the southern reaches of the Indian Ocean, rounded New South Wales, Australia, and turned north-northeast on the long haul across the tropics and the equator to the North Pacific winter. She was scheduled to take on a load of lumber at Hastings Mill in Vancouver and carry it to South Africa. The fates planned otherwise.

One hundred and nine days out from Cape Town, without a stop en route, *Janet Cowan*'s lookouts sighted Cape Flattery off the starboard quarter. The cape is the northwestern extremity of the Olympic Peninsula and is significant for its sharp rock pinnacles standing erect just offshore. The wind at that time was blowing from astern at around 30 miles per hour. As the ship came closer to the land in the middle of the day, the winds slackened. The overcast skies sent rain, and the barometer began to fall. A storm was on its way.

From shore, no more than two miles away, the sailing ship would have been little more than a ghostly speck in the distance, if seen at all. On board, however, the crew were on deck and ready to obey orders. The captain would have been on deck as well when the ship passed Cape Flattery and pointed her bowsprit into Juan de Fuca Strait in the late afternoon. At its mouth, the strait is about 15 miles across: wide enough for most ships in good weather. Hoping for a local pilot or tug, the crew lit her blue lamps, but the worsening weather all but obscured them. In the darkness and the increasing rain, the big sailing ship felt her way east-southeast. On one side stood the Olympic Peninsula, on the other side, Vancouver Island. Neither coast was more than a few miles away, but both were invisible and dangerous.

At about 7:30 p.m. on December 30, the wind abruptly changed. It had been blowing from the southwest, but now came from the east. The barometer continued to fall. Captain Thompson made a quick decision and called for all hands to bring the ship about. That meant turning her through 180 degrees in the middle of the strait. His plan was a sensible one: take *Janet Cowan* back out to the comparative safety of the open sea. Out there, he could sail around at his leisure until the winds proved favourable.

Her progress was quick with the wind on her stern, though she was rigged for a storm under shortened sail. Reports said she carried just topsails, staysails and a storm spanker. Lightly laden, being in ballast, she sat high out of the water, presenting a large area of hull to any contrary wind.

As *Janet Cowan* passed Cape Flattery for the second time that voyage, the easterly wind veered to southerly. The storm increased the current's power, collecting the ship and gradually pushing her to the north-northwest. By this time, judged to be 10 p.m., the seas were getting bigger and the rain had turned to snow. Captain Thompson decided to head for the shelter of Barkley Sound, 40 miles to the northwest.

Without benefit of radar and with virtually no visibility in the combined darkness and snow, it was impossible for the ship's officers to know exactly where they were. They didn't know it, but the wind, driving at them from the southwest and aided by the current, was pushing the ship much too close to land. At midnight, the storm was so intense that the wind sounded like banshees shrieking in the rigging. The wind and waves added thunder to the noise, while the snow and rain made decks slippery. By then, *Janet Cowan* was on a port tack, sailing as close as possible to the wind and desperately trying to maintain sea room. An hour later, the second mate saw a dark shape ahead and raised the alarm: "Land on the starboard bow." That was followed within a few minutes by the most dreaded of cries for sailing ship crews: "Breakers ahead."

The captain called all hands to wear ship, a manoeuvre to claw her away from the land, bringing her on to the opposite tack by turning her in a circular motion, with her stern to the wind for part of that time. The order came too late for the manoeuvre to be completed. As the ship turned stern to the wind, she was driven up onto the shore on a high tide. The surf that early morning was huge. With help from the wind, it lifted the ship and turned her beam on to the sea. She was doomed.

Over the next little while, the surf lifted and pushed the stricken ship so that her bow was wedged among rocks and her stern was caught high on a reef. Between that exposed position and the sheer cliffs that fronted the land was roughly 80 yards of boiling white sea. *Janet Cowan* had run aground just east of Shelter Bight, between Pachena Point and Cape Carmanah.

At daylight, seaman Chamberlain risked his life in the surf to fight his way to land pulling a rope. Although he lost the rope on the way, he was followed by others who managed to get a line ashore. With that in place, they rigged a breeches buoy and hauled the rest of the crew off the ship one by one. Many had had their clothing stripped off by the sea, and they were all frozen. When it came to his turn in the breeches buoy, the captain's hands were so cold that he could not hold on and keep himself upright. Instead, the contraption turned over and dragged him upside down through the surf.

One sailor climbed the cliff and found a telegraph wire. Others soon joined him, and they split into two groups, one following the wire east and the other going west. The remainder of the crew stayed at sea level with the captain, who by then was in serious condition. The eastbound party soon returned, having found no shelter or means of communicating by the wire. Those who went west found a Native shelter, but it was only large enough to hold about half the crew. The rest huddled together on the seashore and tried to keep warm. The icy January wind continued to blow, and snow fell until it was knee-deep.

One day later, the Victoria-based sidewheel steamer *Princess Louise* passed the site in stormy seas. Members of her crew reported seeing a half-submerged ship, with some sails still aloft, on the rocks a few miles east of Pachena Point. Moving in closer, with rescue in mind, lookouts saw no evidence of anyone aboard the wreck, so they assumed all had escaped ashore. *Princess Louise* continued on her voyage to Port Alberni and reported the wreck there.

Two more days passed before another ship sighted the wreck. The American tug *Tyee* was towing a ship to Cape Flattery in much calmer conditions. She immediately dropped her towing line and closed with the shore. Men could be seen on the beach, so the tug launched a boat and headed in. The sight that greeted them was pitiful.

The captain had died of exposure, and another man had gone insane and subsequently died. Two apprentices had also drowned in the surf. Some of the remaining men crouched around a small fire on the beach; others were on the clifftop. They were all more dead than alive. They had been using a tarpaulin as a shelter, but it caught fire and nearly killed even more. Fourteen men were taken off that day to the safety of *Tyee*. A few others, in somewhat better condition in the Native shelter, waited a few days more for *Princess Louise* to return.

Within a very few weeks, nothing remained above the surface of the once-beautiful sailing ship *Janet Cowan*. Over 100 years later, a few rusting relics remain on the seabed as a reminder of her tragic loss.

CHAPTER

6

Cleveland's Fate

THE WINTER AT THE TAIL end of 1897 was reasonably typical
for the west coast from northern California to southern
British Columbia. Storm followed storm in a random
pattern. The SS *Cleveland,* a small iron-hulled steamship
of 730 tons with auxiliary sails, stood at a wharf in San
Francisco being loaded with a cargo of mixed freight and
liquor. It was raining hard, and blustery winds contributed
to the unpleasant conditions. *Cleveland,* formerly named
Sirius, was a veteran of the North Atlantic run between
Nova Scotia and southern Ireland, and she also had served
for a while in the Hawaiian trade. Earlier in 1897, she had
carried passengers and freight to Alaskan ports. She was,
therefore, no stranger to rough seas.

On December 4, the ship cast off her lines and headed out through the Golden Gate to the open sea (the famous bridge of the same name would not be built for another 40 years). The storms had created big swells, and the little ship rolled with the motion, but not enough to alarm those on board.

Off the Columbia River bar on December 6, the main shaft snapped late at night, leaving the ship without engine power. To add to her woes, the foresail had been torn away by the wind earlier. Captain Charles Hall's only hope was that his remaining sails would keep the ship safely offshore while his lookouts kept watch for another ship to take *Cleveland* in tow. After a tense night for all on board, they spoke with the schooner *Marion* heading south. *Marion's* captain agreed to ask any steamer he passed to assist *Cleveland*.

The current and the winds kept the ship moving north through the uncertain days and nights that followed. Two hours after midnight on January 9, lookouts picked up Cape Flattery's welcoming light. No ships had been seen since the schooner three days before. The weather now briefly improved, but then the gale swung round to attack from the northeast. Captain Hall ordered his men to fire distress rockets and flares to catch the attention of the lighthouse keeper or any tugs or other ships in the area. For six hours, the distress signals went off at regular intervals, but no one answered the call for help.

At the mercy of the wind and current, *Cleveland* drifted north across the mouth of Juan de Fuca Strait. In good visibility off Cape Beale, they fired more distress signals. Again, no one answered. The uncontrollable ship passed the cape and drifted along the coast, getter closer to land with each minute. With the breakers pounding on Starlight Reef clearly visible dead ahead, Captain Hall reluctantly gave the order to launch the four lifeboats and abandon ship.

As the boats pulled away, *Cleveland* kept on alone, somehow threading her way through the islands to finally grind ashore on Lyall Point. The four boats carrying the crew became caught up in a current that carried them to the northwest, across the mouth of Barkley Sound. All four boats entered the rough water in Alpha Passage together. Captain Hall's boat, with eight men aboard, made it safely to an island and from there to the mainland. The other three boats disappeared.

Meanwhile, *Cleveland* had been found by local Natives. They looted her, got into the liquor cargo and caused incredible damage to cabins and the ship's equipment. A priest, Reverend Melvin Swarthout, discovered the wreck while the locals were aboard and reported that it was "swarming with Indians who appeared to be raving drunk." In a short time, they had removed an estimated 100 tons of cargo from the wreck.

Three ships searched Barkley Sound for the three missing lifeboats, which between them carried 22 men. The crew of one of the ships, *Willapa*, took time out from the search to remove what was left of the liquor cargo on behalf of the owners. Twelve days after the *Cleveland*'s crew abandoned ship, two of the boats were found. Both had been swept northwest along the coast. One reached shore at Rafael Point, where local Natives found the freezing sailors trying to warm themselves around a beach fire; the other drifted into Hesquiat Harbour. Only one man had been lost from those boats, and he, it was said, had gone insane and died from a combination of hunger and exposure. The fourth boat and the nine men aboard were never seen again.

Despite the damage to her hull caused by the grounding, and that caused inside by the looters, *Cleveland* was not beyond repair. She was 32 years old and partly submerged with gaping holes in her iron hull, but she was not finished. After an inspection by a diver, she was patched where she rested and pulled off the reef by a tug on December 28. She still leaked so badly that she had to be run up on the beach, ending up partly on another reef. Still, she did not die. *Cleveland* had run aground on the British Columbia coast once before, on Trial Island near Victoria, and had survived. She would survive this misfortune too. Once the leaks had been stemmed, two tugs pulled her into deep water and towed her through Juan de Fuca Strait and down Puget Sound to Tacoma. There, she was repaired and again pronounced seaworthy. *Cleveland* was back in business.

Although little is known of her final years, she was

Cape Beale lighthouse was built in 1874 to guide ships to the entrance of Barkley Sound. It stands on a rocky point to mark treacherous reefs. WIKIMEDIA COMMONS

employed for a while as a freighter between San Francisco and Puget Sound. It's probable that she also returned to Alaska, because a photograph from 1901 shows the SS *Cleveland*, a steamship with auxiliary sails, caught fast in ice off the port of Nome. During the days of the Nome gold rush, ships of all sizes and seaworthiness voyaged from San Francisco to the golden Alaskan beaches.

In 1897, however, while *Cleveland* was being pounded by breakers in Barkley Sound, another ship was in trouble in the same general area. The three-masted wooden schooner

Vesta, out of Port Hueneme, California, bound for Port Blakely in Puget Sound, was forced ashore in a storm. *Vesta* was a relatively small ship of only 286 tons, travelling in ballast. Captain Humboldt reported, "We had been fighting a bad storm for several days before reaching Vancouver Island. The weather was thick with the heaviest rain we had ever seen. I thought we were about ten miles south of Cape Flattery when we hit the rocks."

The captain's dead reckoning was a long way off. *Vesta* struck on rocks overshadowed by a high cliff, some nine miles west of the Nitinat River. In an extraordinary stroke of luck for the crew, *Vesta*'s topmasts became caught up in trees on the cliff, creating an excellent escape ladder. The captain recalled, "After going ashore, we were wondering where we were until we found a post on the trail leading nine miles to Carmanah. We took some food ashore and waited two days for help while the sea was rough, then put out in the whaler for the lighthouse."

While the captain and crew were all lucky, *Vesta* was not. She stayed on the rock ledge for a few weeks while the sea pounded at her and broke her apart. The next big storm completed the job and sent what was left to the bottom.

Only a few months later, in the early summer of 1898, a bizarre and completely avoidable accident took place off Cape Beale. The sternwheeler *Marquis of Dufferin* was under tow by the steamer *Progreso*, en route for use on the long Alaskan stretches of the Yukon River. She carried on board a captain and crew of 11, plus an unknown number of male and female passengers. She had been hurriedly built in a Vancouver shipyard earlier that year and fitted with engines and boilers in Victoria. The departure for Alaska was to be her maiden voyage.

Out beyond Juan de Fuca Strait, where the ocean swells rumble over the submerged Swiftsure Bank, the stern-wheeler began to show her deficiencies. In the early hours of the morning, after much less than 24 hours at sea, Captain Connall signalled *Progreso* that he was in serious trouble. He fired distress flares, and the towing ship came alongside to investigate. By that time, the bow was down in the water and breaking apart, the machinery and boilers were coming loose below decks, and the passengers and crew were in fear of their lives.

As the brand new sternwheeler's bow sank and her stern rose high in the air over the rough sea, all on board scrambled down ropes into waiting lifeboats. The heavy, loose machinery broke out of the hull and hurtled to the bottom. The ship, now a useless hulk with only part of its stern visible, drifted away to eventually sink to an unmarked grave. The lifeboats, with frightened but relieved passengers, made slow passage in the dark and stormy seas to the waiting steamer. All on board the *Marquis of Dufferin* were saved, but the voyage could easily have ended in tragedy.

7

The Saga of
King David

KING DAVID IS ONE OF THE most famous heroes from ancient history: the boy warrior who slew the giant Goliath of Gath; the intellectual who ruled a distant land with great wisdom. With a name like *King David,* she should have been invincible.

She (despite the name, the ship was definitely a she) was beautiful. *King David* had long, sleek lines with a proud bowsprit and an elegant fantail. Her deep keel was balanced by three tall, slim masts. Rigged with all sails and flying before the wind, she was a wonderful sight.

This *King David* was Scottish. She was built of iron and steel on the Clyde at Glasgow in 1894 and weighed in at 2,068 tons. Perhaps fittingly, her captain was named

Davidson. Her last port of call, long before reaching the deadly Graveyard, was Salina Cruz, Mexico, on the Gulf of Tehuantepec. She was bound through Juan de Fuca Strait for either Port Townsend or Royal Roads, Victoria.

Considering her destination, *King David* was way off course when she arrived in sight of Vancouver Island. She fetched the land far to the north and west of the strait, off Nootka Sound. By that time, she had been at sea for 116 days, an exceptionally slow voyage for the distance between Salina Cruz and the eastern end of Juan de Fuca Strait. She had, in fact, been posted overdue. To her credit, she had fought hard for northing through a series of violent storms all the way up the coast. She arrived off Nootka Sound on December 10, 1905, in calm but foggy conditions. Captain Davidson reported: "My old charts were out of date and didn't show the latest lights. The first mistake was when I mistook the new lighthouse at Clayoquot for Cape Beale. The weather was thick off the strait and Washington coast, and I had no land observations to correct my course. At 9 p.m. on December 10 the lookout reported breakers on the lee bow, but we cleared them until some more were seen. We weren't sure of our position, so the anchors were let out in only eight fathoms of water."

Davidson's caution was understandable. In the dark of night and additionally hampered by fog, he could have been surrounded by reefs. Anchoring and waiting for daylight or improved conditions was his only safe option. Even so, the waiting would have been hard on everyone's nerves. But wait they did. For two more days, the fog clung to the ship as she strained at her anchor for freedom. Lookouts would have been able to hear heavy surf on the nearby reefs but been unable to see them. The captain had two choices: stay where he was or take to the boats and try to get ashore. He did what all good skippers would do—he stayed with his ship.

On December 13, the fog began to disperse as the wind picked up, blowing from the east-northeast. Now they could see their predicament. Close by, off the lee shore, was a deadly reef. The captain tried to get the anchors up and sail her out to sea, but he was too late. Davidson noted, "The wind increased to the point where the strain was so great that the windlass broke and she was swept onto the rocks. Soon after, she started to break up. A large portion of the bow broke off and was carried by enormous waves high on the rocks. There was little we could do but hold out until the wind and sea subsided, and pray that the ship didn't fall to pieces under our feet."

Captain Davidson did not know that the mountainous seas had thrown *King David* up on Bajo Reef, off the point of the same name. The distance between safety and destruction had been so small. Lost in the fog, the ship had almost cleared the danger, but not quite.

Captain Davidson gathered his papers and gave the order to abandon ship. Twenty-five men took to the boats with him that day and reached shore alive. There was no other sign of life and no way for them to know in which direction to look for rescue. All they could do was look out to sea in the hopes of seeing a passing ship. Had they known where they had run aground, they could have walked to a Native village in less than half a day.

Gathering driftwood, the men built fires on the beach to dry their clothes, keep warm and signal for help. The fires burned day and night, but no one came. When the storm passed, a few men returned to the wreck and brought off all the food and clothing they could find. They found an abandoned shelter nearby and used it for limited protection. The days and nights passed and became a week, then two weeks. Food was running out, and starvation and exposure threatened.

The first officer, a New Zealander named Walstrom, and seven crewmen volunteered to make an attempt to find help by sea. They left in one of the lifeboats on December 23. The boat navigated safely through the surf pounding the reef. Once clear of the land, it turned southeast, heading in the direction of Cape Beale. It was never seen again, and all aboard went missing. Much later came the inevitable theories that the boat had overturned and the men drowned. However, a whaler, or lifeboat, was supposedly found in a sea cave some months later. That boat contained the skeletons of eight men. Could they have been from *King David*? Did they die of exposure before the boat drifted to its enclosed destination? Or was the boat from a completely different wreck? It might also have been a rumour; to this day, that sea cave and the boat with its gruesome cargo have never been found again.

Eighteen men now waited on the beach. All they could do throughout each day was stoke the fires and keep watch for rescue from the sea, but they watched in vain. Starving and getting weaker by the day, they counted the hours as the weeks slowly passed. On January 14, an old sailmaker lost his mind. That same day, a ship passed. Someone aboard the SS *Queen City* noticed smoke from the signal fires on the beach, and the ship sent boats ashore to investigate. The 18 remaining crew members of the barque *King David* were saved. Five days later they arrived in Victoria, where the old sailmaker died.

The crew of *Queen City* couldn't have known it, but they were soon to be involved in another and far greater shipping tragedy on the same coast.

CHAPTER

8

The *Valencia* Tragedy

MANY OF THE WRECKS LITTERING the southwestern coast
of Vancouver Island started their final voyages in San
Francisco. Of all those ill-fated voyages up the west coast,
perhaps the saddest and most catastrophic was that of the
steamer *Valencia*.

There is always a certain hustle and bustle on the wharf
as a ship is readied for departure. It is an exciting time for
passengers and crew heading off for distant ports and for
the uncounted and often unheralded dockworkers who help
load and prepare her for the voyage.

On Saturday, January 20, 1906, the slightly less than
1,600-ton iron steamer *Valencia* rested against Meiggs
Wharf at the Embarcadero. The attractive little ship was

in close view of San Francisco's waterfront streets. Wisps of steam and smoke trailed out of her funnel. A bright sun beamed down on the wharf and on the ship's decks. On board were 104 adult passengers and a few children. Among the adults were 17 women. Sixty-five officers and crew were also aboard to take their charges north on a voyage of only about four days to Victoria and Seattle. Friends and relatives watched from the dock, waving hats and handkerchiefs at those about to leave for the north.

With the echo of the traditional three whistle blasts to signal departure still ringing, Captain Oscar Marcus Johnson gave the order to cast off *Valencia*'s lines at 11:20 a.m. Slowly at first, then gathering speed, the steamer headed out between the Golden Gate headlands to the open ocean.

Valencia was owned by the Pacific Coast Steamship Company. Under a different name, the same group had owned the long-wrecked sidewheeler *Pacific*. *Valencia* had run aground near St. Michael, on Alaska's west coast, by the Yukon River delta. She had also lost deck cargo in a storm. In consequence, she was considered by some among the crew to be an unlucky ship. At least one of them, the cook, had a premonition of disaster before *Valencia* left San Francisco for the last time, yet he sailed anyway.

The official description of the ship included the following: "An iron, single-screw, steam-steering, steam vessel; length 252 feet, beam 34 feet, draft 19 feet without load. She had 3 cargo holds, 4 water-tight metal bulkheads,

2 boilers, with 6 furnaces altogether, and was allowed a steam pressure of 100 pounds." Her cruising speed was said to be 11 knots. Under normal conditions, that would have put her into Victoria, her first scheduled port of call, on the morning of Tuesday, January 23.

All went according to plan for the first 24 hours. *Valencia* steamed up the coast until she passed Cape Mendocino in northern California at 5:30 on Sunday morning. She was then 10 miles offshore. That was the last land reference her crew saw, as the weather then turned. Two official reports said it became "hazy," while others referred to thick fog. Either way, the light at Cape Mendocino was the last to be seen as *Valencia* cruised at her normal speed.

In mid-afternoon on Sunday, the wind changed from a northerly to "a strong breeze from the southeast." According to the second officer, who survived the voyage, Captain Johnson made a notation in the log that the ship passed Cape Blanco, Oregon, at 5:20 p.m. No one else was aware that the cape had actually been seen. The weather continued to deteriorate until by Monday night a fresh gale was blowing and the seas were kicking up rough.

The course that *Valencia* took from off Cape Mendocino to Cape Flattery was on a bearing of approximately north 20° west magnetic to the latitude of the Umatilla Reef lightship off Cape Alaya, Washington. From there, with a slight course correction, it is only 14 miles to Cape Flattery. That course takes ships far enough offshore that they would not normally see interim lights along the Oregon and Washington coasts. The Cape Flattery light should be visible for up to 20 miles out to sea. In addition, the station was equipped with a loud foghorn for murky conditions.

In foggy conditions, before radar and electronic depth sounders, most ships took soundings with a long line and a lead cylinder filled with tallow. Ships closing the region of Umatilla light would do that as a matter of safety, as did *Valencia*. The problem was that *Valencia*'s soundings were started too late. The seabed near Umatilla Reef has peculiarities of depth that would have confirmed the location without doubt. One of the official reports spells it out: "Captain Johnson should have commenced his soundings earlier in the afternoon of Monday, the 22nd, and hauled the ship in until he had from 40 to 50 fathoms, as holding this depth up the Washington coast, the ship could not get across to the Vancouver coast, where similar soundings may be found, without crossing deeper water."

Captain Johnson's soundings showed no bottom at 100 fathoms, therefore, the ship was either too far out to sea, or in a very dangerous location—crossing the entrance to Juan de Fuca Strait. As weather conditions worsened, the captain became concerned. Based on the log line, which trails behind the ship and records her speed through the water, he believed they should be somewhere near Umatilla Reef or Cape Flattery. But he had not taken the north-flowing current into consideration, and he had nothing to show him his actual location. The seas ran high. The fog continued. Running at half speed, *Valencia* rolled unpleasantly. The depth soundings made no sense. The captain rang down for dead slow ahead. Passengers, not aware of the real problem, began to mutter about engine trouble. Six or seven hours after the ship should have passed Cape Flattery, the soundings showed 60 fathoms. That changed rapidly to half that depth. A lookout on the bow gave no hint of danger. However, an officer on the bridge with the captain, 100 feet behind the bow, suddenly saw a black shape dead ahead. He and the captain ordered an immediate turn to the west, but it was too late. A few minutes later, the ship struck a rock. Then she struck another and stopped with a lurch that shook all on board.

"By God! Where are we?" exclaimed Captain Johnson as his ship ran aground.

The immediate reaction by professional seamen when a ship hits something hard is to assess damage. Soundings taken in the bilges of the middle compartment showed *Valencia* had taken in one foot of water in the few minutes since she struck. That quickly increased to two and then to six feet. The ship was sinking. To save her and everyone on board, Johnson ordered the engines full speed astern and ran the wounded ship backwards onto the rocky shore. At the same time, he ordered the lifeboats lowered to the level of the ship's rail and secured there. When she came to rest, *Valencia*'s stern was no more than 250 feet from an almost sheer cliff topped by trees. She could not have found a worse place to hit. Soon after the ship struck, the cook, said to be the survivor of four shipwrecks, was reported to have complained, "I knew it! I have known it all along that she was doomed!"

Although the seas were running high, it should have been possible to launch the lifeboats and, if handled by competent crew, navigate them through the surf to the open sea. From there it would have been possible to find a safe landing place to go ashore. The problem was that no lifeboat drill had taken place. The sailors among the crew who should have handled the boats waited below decks for orders that never came. Passengers and other crew, such as waiters and firemen, lowered the boats to the rails but did not lash them there as ordered. That left the boats much too accessible for some of the passengers to resist. They clambered aboard and, not understanding the correct procedures for lowering the boats into the sea, either hacked through the falls or otherwise released them. This caused three of the loaded boats to nosedive into the water. Only one passenger was rescued. The others drowned in the surf.

Two other boats were launched properly and pulled away from the ship. Unfortunately, they were not adequately crewed by experienced sailors; both soon rolled over in the angry waves. Out of between 20 and 30 people, only nine survived to make their way to the rocks at the base of the cliff. A third boat was also believed to have been launched, but it disappeared without a trace.

SS *Valencia* ran out of sea room in January 1906. Instead of cruising through Juan de Fuca Strait, she crashed into the rocky shore of Vancouver Island with a huge loss of life.

On the ship, the remaining passengers and crew took refuge in the dining salon. At that time, it was estimated that 110 people were still on board. They still didn't know where they were. The captain believed they had struck somewhere south of Cape Flattery. No one knew they were on Vancouver Island. Throughout that night, the crew fired off distress rockets without attracting any attention. One rocket exploded as it was lit and broke the captain's hand.

The nine men who had reached shore spent a miserable night on the rocks about 500 yards west of the wreck. At daybreak, they climbed the cliff and found a telegraph line. Assuming they were somewhere south of Cape Flattery, they followed the line to the west in the expectation of finding assistance.

Meanwhile, back on the wreck, Captain Johnson called for volunteers to take the last lifeboat along the coast to look for a safe landing place. From there, they were to force a way through the dense brush on the cliffs to a point opposite *Valencia*'s stern and then fire a light line across the intervening water. Using the line, the men could haul over a heavy-duty rope and secure it to trees. With that in place, everyone on board could have crossed one at a time in a breeches buoy.

Seven men volunteered for the task under boatswain McCarthy. The boat was lowered with precision and, the men rowing hard, successfully crossed the breakers beyond the ship's bow and turned to the west. After approximately seven miles, they were able to go ashore on the west side of Pachena Bay. The time was between noon and 1:00 p.m.

However, the plan began to fall apart. Instead of fighting back through the bushes and trees to get behind the wreck as ordered, McCarthy and his men found the telegraph line and a sign that read, "Three miles to Cape Beale." That told them they were on Vancouver Island and that a lighthouse was nearby. They turned west and delivered news of the wreck at 3:00 p.m. The other men on shore had found a lineman's hut and telegraph equipment, so were able to send a message to the lighthouse at Carmanah, also in the middle of Tuesday afternoon. Those two events set in motion the rescue by sea. But it was already too late.

On board *Valencia*, the crew had not been idle. They set up the line-firing gun and, after a couple of failed attempts, managed to send a line into the trees up on the cliff. All they needed was for one of the shore parties to return and haul over the heavy rope. They waited and waited, but no one showed up. The thin line began to sag until it dipped into the sea and became caught on debris from the ship. Before long it was cut through.

Through all this, over 100 passengers and crew still on board watched the water creeping higher and higher. Big waves kept breaking over the bow and washed away much of the superstructure. Two men, an officer and a fireman, tried to swim ashore to connect a line. Neither of them could get through the surf, and both had to be pulled back to the ship. As night fell, some of the survivors gathered on the hurricane deck in the freezing rain. Others climbed into the rigging in a vain attempt to stay out of the water. They were there all night and into Wednesday morning. Exposed to the wind and sea, and terribly cold, they must have thought the night would go on forever.

At 9:30 on Wednesday morning, someone saw a ship. She was the SS *Queen City*, which had been dispatched from Victoria to attempt a rescue. Only one week before, the crew of *Queen City* had recovered the captain and crew of the square-rigger *King David* from Bajo Point at Nootka Sound. Now she was again on the scene of a shipwreck. *Queen City* stopped less than two miles away from where *Valencia* lay on the rocks, but she did not lower any boats this time. The *Valencia* crew hurriedly launched two life rafts. At the same time, the line-firing gun was fired a few times to attract attention. Ten men rowed the first raft out through the breakers but could not reach the rescue ship. They drifted west with the current until late at night. When the raft made the shore on Turret Island, 17 miles away from the wreck, only nine men were still alive. Five of those soon went out of their minds and jumped into the sea, where they drowned. The remaining four were subsequently rescued by the steamer *Salvor*.

The second raft was tied alongside *Valencia*. The ship's officers tried to persuade the women to board the raft and make for the distant *Queen City*. They refused, probably expecting boats to come for them soon. Instead, 18 men—the maximum it could handle—rowed and paddled the raft out to sea.

Another ship, the SS *City of Topeka*, was also out looking for the wreck and for survivors. While no one aboard *Queen City* apparently saw either of the rafts, *Topeka* did later pick up the 18 men. Both rescue ships, incidentally, belonged to the same company as *Valencia*. Once *Topeka* was in position, although not able to see the wreck, *Queen City* was ordered to leave the scene and resume her voyage.

Two other vessels came close that day. The small Canadian ships *Salvor* and *Czar* did not remain long at the scene, although *Czar* did go in close. They both steamed away to Bamfield, planning to organize a rescue team to approach the wreck by land.

It must have been heartbreaking for the freezing passengers and crew on *Valencia* to see salvation so close, only to watch three of the four ships steam away. Due to the poor weather, *Topeka*'s crew did not actually see *Valencia* at any time. They knew she was nearby, and they went in close to the coast and patrolled east and west a few miles, but could not find her. She was in dire straits, gradually being broken up by the violent seas.

While the strange events took place at sea, three men arrived on the cliffs. They had come from Carmanah lighthouse in response to the telegraph message. They found the remnants of the line fired ashore earlier and could see the ship on the rocks. As they watched, helpless, the ship broke apart, tossing all on board into the sea. They all appeared to be wearing lifejackets, but the sea drowned many, beat some to death on the rocks and carried others out to the breakers. Having already been exposed to the dreadful weather for some 36 wintry hours, they would have succumbed quickly to the icy water.

All the women on board *Valencia* died in the sea that day, as did the children and most of the male passengers. Also lost were the captain and 39 of the officers and crew. Only 12 passengers and 25 crew members lived to tell their version of those terrifying few days.

CHAPTER

9

Soquel's Misfortune

THREE YEARS AFTER THE *VALENCIA* tragedy, another ship lost its way in bad weather in the Graveyard of the Pacific. The American-registered, four-masted wooden schooner *Soquel*, weighing 767 tons, left Callao, Peru, on December 11, 1908. She was in ballast and bound non-stop for Port Townsend, Washington. *Soquel's* demise was the result of a series of accidents that would have appeared almost slapstick if they had not been so tragic.

On January 22, 1909, in a snowstorm and high winds, *Soquel* arrived off the mouth of Juan de Fuca Strait. On board were Captain Charles Henningsen, his wife and three-year-old daughter, plus a crew of 12. The long voyage from the southern hemisphere had been routine, and everyone on board was looking forward to getting into port in a few hours.

Through the gloom, a light could be seen off *Soquel*'s starboard bow. The captain decided it was the Cape Flattery light and set a course to take his ship into the strait. Before he knew what was happening, *Soquel* ran up onto Seabird Rocks, at the entrance to Pachena Bay on Vancouver Island. He was 30 miles northwest of where he expected to be. Somehow, probably due to faulty navigation by dead reckoning, Henningsen had missed Cape Flattery completely and mistaken the light from Pachena Point for the light on Tatoosh Island. The three main Seabird Rocks, named for their breeding colonies of auks, cormorants and gulls, stand guard at the entrance to Pachena Bay.

Big waves pounded the schooner and pushed her over the first rock and far up on the others. The initial crash woke Mrs. Henningsen, who was in bed in the master's cabin. Although her husband called down and ordered her to stay below, she dressed quickly, wrapped a blanket around her child and went on deck. For some reason, the furled sails had been let down. Flapping wildly, they would have added to the general air of noise and confusion. The foresail blew away while the captain was busy helping crew members prepare a lifeboat. Taking his daughter in his arms, he helped his wife into the boat. The schooner hung there on the rocks, swinging crazily from side to side and banging her keel up and down as the seas smashed into her hull.

A comber broke hard against the ship, causing it to roll almost onto its beam, and Mrs. Henningsen cried to her husband, "This is death: kiss me, Carl." He did so and was about to hand the child to her mother when the storm snapped the mizzen and jigger masts and brought them crashing down. A spar hit the captain's daughter on the head and crushed her skull, killing her instantly and tearing her from the captain's arms. It also knocked him off his feet and injured his back. The end of the same spar swung down to kill his wife and wreck the lifeboat.

The crew were in a panic by this time. While the dazed captain staggered to his feet, some ran about the ship screaming with fear. None responded to orders, if they even heard them above the noise of the storm. The first mate launched another boat, and he and five men got away from the ship to a large rock nearby, where they spent the night in the open.

On *Soquel*, some semblance of order had been restored by the grief-stricken captain. Despite that, several times through the long night hours he had to persuade men not to launch another boat. Such a manoeuvre, he told them, would surely result in their deaths. Two sailors climbed up on the spinnaker boom in a futile attempt to get above the breaking waves. The boom snapped, and they fell to the steeply canted deck, causing one of them to break his leg.

The steamer *Leebro* came in sight out of Bamfield at 10:00 a.m. The first of two rescue ships to arrive on the

Soquel ran aground on Seabird Rocks, close to the entrance to Barkley Sound, in January 1909. Two members of the captain's family died. ROYAL BC MUSEUM, BC ARCHIVES B-00455

scene, it could do nothing at first. Big seas ran in from the southwest and broke over the stranded schooner. The sailors on board *Leebro* could only watch and wait. At about 1:30 p.m., she was joined by another steamer, the SS *Tees*, which had come from Victoria. The seas were still too rough to attempt a rescue, and both ships had to stand off until conditions improved later in the afternoon. At 4:00 p.m., the combined resources of the two steamers managed, with great difficulty, to take five sailors off the other rock, leaving only the mate, Mr. Swanson. He refused to leave while his captain and crew were still in danger.

Much to the distress of *Soquel*'s crew, *Leebro* and *Tees* left for Bamfield as darkness fell; they could do nothing more until daylight. Another ship, the US Coast Guard's *Manning*, arrived and illuminated the wreck with its searchlight. That vessel's captain had heard the news of the shipwreck by radio from Victoria. As the tide fell, the space between the wreck of the schooner and the rock where Swanson waited alone dried out. Aided by the beam of light, everyone left *Soquel* with as much food as they could carry and joined Swanson on his lonely rock. Many crew members coming off the ship were injured, but were helped away by their shipmates. In the end, only the bodies of the captain's wife and daughter remained on board.

At daybreak, with a definite improvement in the weather, *Manning*'s crew were able to launch a boat and take off the 13 sailors. Members of the Wyadda Island (Washington) lifeboat crew were on board *Manning*. Four of them risked their own lives to retrieve the two bodies from *Soquel*. The next morning, they returned to the wreck and took away the captain's personal papers, including his master's certificate, his navigation instruments and some of his wife's jewellery, which were all returned to him.

Soquel stayed on Seabird Rocks, regularly battered by waves, until the next storm broke her up and carried the debris out to sea.

10

The Deadly Storms
of Early 1923

JANUARY AND FEBRUARY 1923 ARE remembered for a series of deadly storms. The lighthouse keepers along the coast of Vancouver Island claimed that these two months brought the worst weather they had experienced for many, many years. For ships going in or out of the confined Juan de Fuca Strait, the storms created nightmares of enormous proportions. They also caused desperate situations for the personnel of the undermanned and overworked rescue stations.

The new year was only 12 hours old when *Alaskan* slipped her lines in Victoria. She was just a little ship, a wooden steamer less than 100 feet long and 19 feet wide and registered at a mere 150 tons. Having just taken on a cargo of salt for Barkley Sound, Captain Baillies and his crew of 10 men were looking forward to a short voyage of less than 24 hours. There were probably a few hangovers among the crew after the New Year's Eve festivities ashore, but the clean, salty air would soon blow those cares away.

The weather wasn't good, but about normal for the season and location. *Alaskan*'s bow carved through the waters of the strait and took her to the herring fisheries of Barkley Sound without incident. There she unloaded and probably took on a cargo of salted fish before heading back to Victoria. The seas were much rougher when she left again; the first storm of the year had begun its attack on the coast.

On shore, the keeper of the Pachena Point lighthouse watched as *Alaskan* fought her way out of the sound and into the big seas. She was having a hard time of it, but at first appeared to be making headway. By mid-afternoon, with the light failing, the little ship was in trouble. Something had gone wrong on board—perhaps it was her steering mechanism, or possibly engine failure. The light keeper saw her drifting outside Pachena Bay, apparently out of control and dangerously close to Seabird Rocks. As night fell, she vanished in the darkness.

The telegraph lines between Pachena Point and Bamfield were down that day, so the light keeper could not report what he had seen to the rescue station. On the morning of January 3, flares were seen from near Seabird Rocks. The Bamfield station sent a team out to help. They found little at first, seeing no wreckage. After searching for a while, they found a body wearing a lifejacket marked *Alaskan*. The dead man was floating in big waves just west of Pachena Point. Then a lifeboat was found on a beach nearby. It carried lifejackets marked *Alaskan* and other items, but no survivors. There was no doubt that the little steamer had gone to her final resting place on the seabed, but no one knew where. It was assumed she had run up on Seabird Rocks and then been dragged off again by the undertow to sink in deep water, taking all hands with her except one lone body. That was the first loss of the year.

The British freighter *Tuscan Prince* spent less than a decade at sea. Built and launched at Sunderland, England, in 1913, she was registered as 5,275 gross tons. She was 420 feet in length with a beam of 54 feet. Her cruising speed was said to be 12 knots. *Tuscan Prince* began her career with the Prince Line in December 1913 and almost made it through the four years of the First World War without damage. Then a U-boat put a torpedo into her in the English Channel on August 5, 1918, just a few months before the war ended. Although she was holed, her crew got her to a friendly port for repairs.

Four years after the end of the war, *Tuscan Prince*, commanded by Captain Chilvers, let go her lines at Market Street and steamed out of San Francisco Bay. Unlike so many other ships that came to grief on Vancouver Island, however, she was not bound through Juan de Fuca Strait. Her destination was Port Alberni, up a deep inlet on the west coast of Vancouver Island. She was scheduled to load lumber from the mill there.

On St. Valentine's Day, 1923, she came up toward Cape Flattery in a blinding snowstorm and howling gale. It was night, and the light should have been visible, but it was not seen. One of the crew later said they had not seen any lights since leaving San Francisco, due to the weather. That night, unsure of his location, Captain Chilvers had his ship running at slow speed, intending to be off Cape Beale in daylight.

That was a bad week for deadly storms in the Pacific Northwest. Four ships came to grief off the entrance to Juan de Fuca Strait within as many days. On Monday, February 12, the American motor ship *Coolcha*, inbound from San Francisco like so many others, lost her way in a storm in the strait and fetched up on an exposed reef at Albert Head, near Victoria. Pounded by huge waves, she tried to back off the rocks at high tide but only succeeded in getting holed and jammed broadside to the coast. The storm-driven waves turned her into a complete wreck. Some time later, a radio message relayed via Victoria announced that *Coolcha* had been abandoned and her crew rescued by the salvage steamer *Algerine*.

The steamer *Nika*, outbound with a load of lumber from Port Gamble on Puget Sound for a California destination, lost her propeller off Umatilla Reef. Drifting helplessly in mountainous waves, she somehow caught fire. A station in

Walla Walla, Washington, picked up her distress call and passed it on. Once more out of the west came a faint SOS and a call saying, "We are on fire. Help!" But there was no signature. Then the operator at the naval radio station at Bremerton, Washington, reported that he thought he "heard *Nika* say something about fire aboard but couldn't understand it all." The operator at the Smith Island radio compass station reported less kindly: "Apparently inexperienced operator on watch."

Nika's crew were fortunate that another ship had seen her and also reported the fire by radio. The US Coast Guard cutter *Snohomish*, commanded by Captain R.R. Waesche, was in Port Angeles. He radioed, "We are going to aid steamer *Nika*, reported lost rudder, dangerous position off Umatilla Reef." From Port Angeles to Umatilla Reef was an estimated eight hours' voyage. The *Snohomish* searched for the burning ship and at first reported no progress. Meanwhile, the steamer *Kewanee*, off the entrance to Juan de Fuca Strait, saw a glare, which was assumed to be a ship on fire.

Santa Rita got into the act too. She was a steel steamer of 1,600 tons. Hearing the radio chatter, she broke in at 3:00 a.m. to advise that she could be on the scene in an hour. To Captain Waesche's credit, *Snohomish* found the burning ship and took off her crew. He radioed, "Rescued total crew of thirty-four men from burning Nika. Now standing by wreck. Will give obstruction report later." In his more detailed report, he said, "The sea was too rough for lowering of boats so Snohomish put bow up close along stern burning Nika and took crew off with improvised breeches buoy, men putting buoy on and jumping into water and being hauled aboard. Heat intense. No one lost, three men slightly hurt."

Nika was too far gone to save, though. Still on fire, she was left to drift. The coastal passenger steamer *Princess Maquinna* saw her and reported that she was half submerged. Beyond hope, *Nika* continued to burn and drifted away. She is believed to have sunk somewhere off Ucluelet.

St. Valentine's Day proved an unhappy one for the *Santa Rita* as well as the British *Tuscan Prince*. *Santa Rita* was looking for Juan de Fuca Strait in the same snowstorm. She never did find the burning *Nika*. The winds and current forced her off course, and an hour after her message about *Nika*, she slammed into a rocky promontory near Clo-oose, a Native village by Nitinat Inlet. A desperate message went out over her radio: "We are breaking up fast; we are going to drown." The radio then went dead for a while, and no position report could be given. Then she came back on the air briefly. "Santa Rita, off Tatoosh on rocks, sinking, receiver broken, cannot hear anyone. Captain says she won't sink but the water is rough. Asks if anyone on the way."

Despite repeated attempts, no ship or shore station could raise her, and ships that went looking for her failed to sight the wreck. Her crew, however, were luckier than many who became wrecked on the deadly coastline. *Santa Rita* ended

The British freighter *Tuscan Prince* ended her career on Village Island in Barkley Sound on February 14, 1923. VANCOUVER MARITIME MUSEUM

up close to shore and had aboard a sailor who happened to be not only brave but a powerful swimmer as well. Towing a heavy line, he fought his way in icy water, over rocks and through breaking waves to the beach. There he fastened the line to a large rock, and his shipmates were able to come across one by one in the breeches buoy. Until the storm blew itself out, they sheltered in a lineman's hut before reaching Clo-oose. *Santa Rita* did not survive the storm. That night, coastal winds gusted to over 70 mph and tore her apart, with help from the waves. Her crew were picked up by the US Coast Guard vessel *Algonquin* and delivered safely to Port Angeles, Washington.

Tuscan Prince came to grief about the same time as *Santa Rita*. She plowed into rocks with her bow close to a rocky point on Village Island in Barkley Sound. A Seattle newspaper erroneously reported that she had gone ashore and was a total loss on Estevan Point in Nootka Sound. That location report apparently came from the US Coast Guard ship *Algonquin*. *Tuscan Prince*'s radio operator sent out the message, "SOS Tuscan Prince ashore at—," before the radio failed. All the lights on the ship went out at the same time. Huge combers swept over the stern, flooding the engine room and radio shack. The crew climbed up into the bow, which was held high by the rocks, and sheltered there.

Tuscan Prince, like *Santa Rita*, had a powerful swimmer among the crew. He got ashore with a line and helped rig a breeches buoy. All crew members were then taken off the ship safely, but they were still stranded. When daybreak gave enough light, the captain and a few others used the fixed rope to return to the ship and collect food. All were rescued by a professional lifeboat crew from Bamfield later that day.

Efforts were made to salvage *Tuscan Prince*, but they were unsuccessful. Most of her cargo was recovered, but repeated southwesterly gales pounded her hull for the next two months. Badly holed in too many places, she broke up and slipped off the rocks into deeper water.

11

Tatjana's Plight

THE NORWEGIAN STEAMER *TATJANA* FOLLOWED *Tuscan Prince* to her grave one year later. Built in Montreal, *Tatjana* was a similar size at 5,329 tons. She was 400 feet long and had a beam of 52 feet.

Unlike *Tuscan Prince*, which departed from San Francisco on her final voyage, *Tatjana* sailed out of Muroran, Japan, in ballast. She too was due to pick up a load of good British Columbia lumber, but from Vancouver. The long crossing of the North Pacific went without a hitch, although they had to run through a winter storm. Three days out from Cape Flattery, the late February weather turned against them.

Captain Norvig was an experienced sailor. He knew only

too well the harsh reputation of the coastal waters ahead. As the weather thickened, he reduced speed and called for soundings. Lookouts on the bow were warned to watch for coastal lights and listen for foghorns. They saw nothing and heard not a sound, other than the breaking seas and the ship's deep breathing.

Near midnight on February 26, with no land references, no lights and no foghorns blaring their lonely messages, Norvig was told the depth under the ship was 45 fathoms. That told him *Tatjana* was coming up toward land, but he had no idea whether it was the Washington coast or Vancouver Island. The snow was falling heavily, and as the temperature plummeted, ice began to form in the rigging and on the mast and decks.

On the bow, face frozen and eyes half-closed to keep out the gritty snow, the lookout saw breakers just off to port. He yelled the alarm, and the captain responded with the order for full steam ahead and an immediate turn to starboard. It takes time for a ship to come about onto a new course—too much time when danger threatens. Before *Tatjana* could get clear of the reef and find deep water, her stern hit. The propeller, spinning at full revolutions, was broken off by the impact, and the rudder sustained damage. Unable to answer her helm without the rudder and unable to steam to safety without the propeller to drive her through the water, *Tatjana* was forced up onto rocks in a small cove on the east shore of Effingham Island. She immediately began to take on water.

Tatjana lost her direction in dreadful weather conditions in late February 1924. She went ashore in Barkley Sound, but was eventually refloated and repaired. VANCOUVER MARITIME MUSEUM

As so often happened with ships aground on the Vancouver Island coast, the *Tatjana*'s crew did not know where they were. The radioed distress call told listeners only that they thought they were on Carmanah Point. Tugs immediately set out from Victoria and Seattle. Standing at Bamfield, in Barkley Sound, the Royal Canadian Navy trawler *Armentières* set sail to join the search. At roughly the same time, the Bamfield lifeboat went out, with the highly experienced coxswain Percy Brady at the helm.

Fortunately for the stranded crew and for those out looking for the ship, *Tatjana*'s radio officer sent out a later message. This time he advised that the ship was flooding and would soon be without power. That was enough for the radio operator at Bamfield. He took a fix on the message and was able to establish her location as Barkley Sound, not near Carmanah Point. Still searching for the ship in daylight, Coxswain Brady saw a patch of oil in the sound. The men on *Armentières* found oil in the sound too.

While rescuers searched, *Tatjana*'s crew were saving themselves. During the night, one brave soul volunteered to take a line ashore. It wasn't far, but the surf was horrendous over the rocks, and reports told of a "vicious undertow." Somehow the crewman made it to shore and climbed as high as he could before anchoring his line securely to the cliff. He was followed by others, pulling themselves hand over hand from the ship to the cliff. The weak of heart stayed where they were until morning, preferring the doubtful security of the wrecked ship to the danger of the short rope crossing. Once it was light, they too found extra courage and took deep breaths before swinging ashore.

With the radio fix and the oil to guide them, Brady and his team found *Tatjana* early in the afternoon of February 27. She was down by the stern so deeply that the waves washed over the rear half of her decks. Brady's boat ferried six of the wrecked crew to Bamfield. The others stood by their ship, hoping she could yet be saved. Later that day, they too left her.

Surprisingly, *Tatjana* did not sink. She was caught fast

and stuck to the island for weeks. After a lot of hard and dangerous work, salvagers managed to pump her out, patch her up and refloat her. She was then towed to Victoria for substantial repairs. When she emerged from dry dock the following summer, she had a new name: *Drammensfjord*.

While *Tatjana* submitted to the shipyard workers in Victoria, the next winter brought more storms and more suffering for ships and sailors. One incident was unusual for the region, as it involved a crew more conditioned to the warm waters of the South Seas than the cold of the northwest.

On January 17, 1925, the 300-ton wooden schooner *Raita* was towed out of Seattle Harbour by a tug. Under the command of Captain Jean Louis Richam, her crew of Polynesian sailors set *Raita's* sails once she cleared navigational hazards. She was carrying a cargo of lumber on deck and was bound for Papeete, Tahiti.

It's probable that the schooner had not been well maintained by her French owner in Tahiti. The big waves in Juan de Fuca Strait pounded her hull and opened up a few seams. A trickle of water became a stream, and soon the pumps could not keep up with the flow. *Raita* turned in her own wake and headed for the sanctuary of a port.

A southeast gale blew in overnight and aided the waves in pounding the endangered vessel. She took on more water than the pumps could handle and settled lower and lower in the water. The crew had done all they could. A few miles off Carmanah Point, they dropped two anchors in a vain attempt to hold the schooner, but the winds were too strong and the sea too rough. Pushed by the wind, *Raita* dragged her anchors. The already exhausted crew of 10 took to a lifeboat and risked their lives anew in the surf to reach the lighthouse.

Raita, which had found a modicum of fame when a Polynesian sea mound was named after her in 1921, took a merciless beating from the northern sea and broke up in huge waves. What was left of her and her cargo came ashore off the village of Clo-oose. Other debris drifted up Nitinat Inlet. At least there was some good news: all the crew survived and went home to their island paradise.

CHAPTER

12

Naval Ships at Risk

IT'S NOT OFTEN THAT ONE comes across mention of military vessels in the tales of shipwrecks in the notorious Graveyard of the Pacific. Yet a few British, American and Canadian naval ships have met disaster in this dangerous region.

On either December 2 or 3, 1901, Britain's Royal Navy lost HMS *Condor* somewhere off Tatoosh Island. *Condor* was hit by a hellish storm soon after leaving Esquimalt, BC, bound for Hawaii. She was a steel sloop of war built on the Thames estuary only three years before. Stationed on Vancouver Island for a while, she was acknowledged to be fast and extremely seaworthy. In the cold, wet and windy winter of 1901, her complement of 130 officers and men, and possibly 10 naval cadets, would have been looking forward to their time in the tropical sun. The 180-foot-long ship, powered by triple-expansion engines and aided when necessary by auxiliary sails, raced out through Juan de Fuca Strait to the Pacific Ocean at the beginning of December.

Condor passed Tatoosh Island and left Cape Flattery light behind, signalling her farewell to the land. Late that night, one of the worst storms in living memory blasted the Pacific Northwest. HMS *Condor*, built to withstand extreme conditions, disappeared with every member of her crew and without leaving a trace. Another Royal Navy ship, HMS *Warspite*, had left Esquimalt with *Condor*, but she delayed in the strait, apparently for gunnery practice. When she emerged onto the ocean in the aftermath of the storm, she met seas like mountains and high winds. *Warspite* suffered damage, but managed to weather the tempest. Had her captain not chosen to exercise his gunnery crews, she too would almost certainly have joined *Condor* in a fight for survival against the elements or, at worst, descended to the seabed.

Another ship was in the area at the time that *Condor* disappeared. The 3,300-ton steel freighter *Matteawan* had been sighted passing Cape Flattery the day before the naval ship. Loaded with 5,000 tons of coal from Nanaimo, she also disappeared, leaving nothing to show where she went down.

In the late 1920s, the Royal Canadian Navy owned a fleet of 12 battle-class steel trawlers. Four of them were employed as protection vessels for the Department of Marine and

Fisheries, patrolling the coasts of British Columbia. One was named HMCS *Thiepval*. She was 130 feet long and 25 feet in width.

Thiepval was launched for the Royal Canadian Navy at Kingston, Ontario, on the eastern end of Lake Ontario, in 1917. For the final months of the First World War, she worked off Newfoundland as a guard for trans-Atlantic convoys. Coal-fired, her maximum speed of 10 knots would not allow her to serve in any other capacity, although she did hunt U-boats without success. In March 1920, she was loaned to the Department of Marine and Fisheries as a patrol vessel and sent to the west coast by way of the Panama Canal. *Thiepval*'s first years in the Pacific Northwest kept her crew busy. She hit bottom near Prince Rupert in 1920 and did the same near Bella Bella a year later. She was lucky each time, getting away with a few scrapes and bruises and minor leaks.

At the tail end of winter 1924, she crossed the North Pacific to Hakodate, Japan. Her task was to place fuel and oil dumps for a round-the-world flight attempt by British military aviators. Squadron Leader Stuart MacLaren and Flying Officer Plenderleith did not succeed in their attempt. They wrecked the aeroplane (a Vickers Vulture flying boat) that August at Nikolski, in the Komandorski Islands. *Thiepval* went to salvage the wreckage. That short stay made her the first Canadian warship to visit any part of the new Communist Russia.

Back in British Columbia after her foreign adventures, *Thiepval* took on the roles of fisheries protection vessel and lifeguard. Each winter, she and the others of her class went on three-week "Life Saving Patrols" along the west coast of Vancouver Island. She even rescued her sister ship HMCS *Armentières*, which hit a rock in Barkley Sound. Between patrols, the crews laid over at Bamfield, so they were close and ready for action when required. *Thiepval*'s radio room was manned and operational 24 hours a day in case a ship needed assistance. In one rescue, she assisted the Mexican schooner *Chapultepec* by pulling her off a reef at Carmanah Point in 1926.

The waters of Barkley Sound claimed *Thiepval* when she was returning from a patrol under the command of Lieutenant Commander Harold Tingley. Heading for Bamfield in the early afternoon of February 27, 1930, Tingley cut through the Broken Islands at near high tide. As he had done before, he used a broad channel between Turret and Turtle islands. Running at nine knots, *Thiepval* was scored by a submerged but uncharted rock, and she was brought to a standstill. She sent out a distress signal, and HMCS *Armentières* raced from Victoria to help.

Tingley calmly went about the process of examining his ship. He stopped the engines and had all hatches battened down. Finding no obvious life-threatening damage, he tried to take her off using full astern power. The propeller lashed the water to foam, but *Thiepval* would not move. He ordered

HMCS *Thiepval* impaled herself on a rock in Barkley Sound
while returning to Bamfield from a patrol along the west coast of
Vancouver Island. She eventually slid off the rock into deep water.
DEPARTMENT OF NATIONAL DEFENCE, MC-10041

an inspection of the ship from the water, having a boat lowered to cruise right round her. The report came back that
she was sitting with her forward section lodged on a rock
shelf. Tingley watched the rising tide, hoping it would help
float her off. It did not.

When the tide changed and went on the ebb, the trawler's
position became potentially dangerous. She was listing so
far that Tingley had the stokers shift coal from the low side
of the ship to the high side. He had the crew take a cable
across to Turtle Island and secure it there in an attempt to
keep *Thiepval* upright. Close to 5 p.m., with the tide still on
the ebb, the ship lurched to starboard at 45 degrees. Soon

after, Tingley ordered his 21-man crew to abandon ship. They rowed the short distance to Turtle Island and made camp for the night where they could continue to keep a watch on their ship.

Armentières arrived at daybreak, and the two crews witnessed a sad and sorry sight: *Thiepval* was laid over at 60 degrees with her stern underwater. Tingley and members of his crew, however, went back aboard the ship for another inspection and found the engine room flooded and the water rising to the mess deck. Accepting the situation was out of their control, Tingley ordered his shipmates to carry off everything of value. As they left, the sea was already beginning to flow over the starboard gunwale.

With no other option, the naval authorities sent for a salvage ship, aptly named *Salvage King*, but she did not get there in time. Long before the salvagers arrived, *Thiepval* lost her balance on the rock in the dark of night and slipped off into deep water, where she still lies.

The US Navy lost one of their older troopships off Tatoosh Island in January 1972. The 11,828-ton USS *General M.C. Meigs* was under tow by the US Navy tug *Gear* from Olympia, Washington, to San Francisco. A Force 8 gale blew in, hitting the tug and tow with high winds and big seas. At 3:00 a.m. on January 9, the tow line parted west of Cape Flattery, and *General M.C. Meigs* was free, dangerous and in peril. The tug and US Coast Guard vessels worked together to harness the drifting 622-foot-long ship, but without success.

USS *General M.C. Meigs* off the US east coast in July 1944. The former troopship was under tow off Cape Flattery in January 1972 when the tow line parted in a storm. She drifted ashore and broke in three. US NATIONAL ARCHIVES, #80-G-235158

While they stood by helplessly, the wind and waves carried the big grey ship to land until she struck a rocky ledge and broke in two, with the halves wrapped around a big rock pinnacle. She came to rest in full view of the mainland, only seven miles south of Cape Flattery. Her shattered remains are there to this day.

13

Nereus and
Pass of Melfort

ORIGINALLY NAMED *PFALZ* WHEN SHE was launched in Germany in 1913, the 6,570-ton steel freighter was renamed *Boorara* by new owners in 1915. In 1926, she was sold to a Greek shipowner who renamed her *Nereus* in honour of the sea god from Greek mythology.

Nereus left Kobe, Japan, in mid-July 1937, to collect a cargo of lumber from Port Alberni, BC. The long crossing of the North Pacific was uneventful. The latter part of the voyage, which should have taken the freighter through Barkley Sound and all the way up the Alberni Inlet to its head, would have been a pleasure cruise through magnificent Vancouver Island scenery.

The Greek ship arrived off Vancouver Island on Sunday

morning, August 8, 1937. After the constant rolling swells of the ocean, the coastal waters were calm, but fog shrouded much of the land. Captain John Kalalanos delivered his charge to the entrance of Barkley Sound with professional navigational skill. But he was not quite on course, perhaps due to the fog that lay heavy over the sound and its many islands. Expecting to pick up a local pilot from the Bamfield station, Captain Kalalanos entered what he thought was the sound. Had he been a little farther to the northwest, he would have been safe. Instead, at 7:20 a.m., *Nereus* drove up on the rocks.

The ship's momentum and the action of the sea turned her beam onto the reef, and a sharp rock ruptured her hull, forcing its pinnacle into the engine room. Although the sea was calm, there is always movement on open shores. The ship had come to rest on an even keel, but the waves rolled *Nereus* back and forth on the rocks, tearing off her rudder and sternpost. Her tortured metal screamed and groaned as the rocks ground into her hull. Water streamed in to flood her interior from a variety of wounds.

When rescue craft came out from Bamfield, they found the crew had launched a lifeboat with 28 men aboard. It was soon towed in to safety. The fog dispersed, showing the ship's location as about half a mile from Cape Beale lighthouse. She could hardly have found anywhere more dangerous to hit. On one side was the open sea with its sudden and unpredictable storms, which happen in summer as well as in winter, though not with the same frequency or severity. The extended reef that *Nereus* hit is notorious for strong currents, riptides and sharp rocks and is the primary reason for the lighthouse's existence.

With most of the crew taken off, Captain Kalalanos and five of his officers stayed on board for a while, believing the ship was stable enough to remain where she was for some time. Their dedication was admirable but futile, as salvage experts soon confirmed. Finally convinced that they could do no more for her, the captain and his officers left the ship for the last time. While attempted salvage operations were under way, heavy seas worked at the wreck, breaking her in two and casting her remains into deep water.

The master of *Nereus* was not alone in wrecking his ship at the entrance to Barkley Sound. Thirty-two years before, at Christmas 1905, the Scottish four-masted barque *Pass of Melfort* went violently aground at Amphitrite Point, on the opposite side of the sound, near Ucluelet. Not much is known of the 2,200-ton sailing ship, except that she was built in Glasgow in 1891 and carried a crew of either 27 or 35, depending on the storyteller. A *New York Times* article of December 29, 1905, with a Victoria, BC, dateline, stated 27 people died, including one woman.

The big windship, with Captain H. Scougall in charge, sailed from Panama in ballast and was bound for Port Townsend, Washington. Although it has not been confirmed, the woman on board was probably Captain Scougall's wife.

Somewhere near Cape Flattery, the ship was hit by a southeast gale and driven northwest to her destruction on the rocks. The last ship to see *Pass of Melfort* was another British vessel, *Brodrick Castle*, which reported her near Juan de Fuca Strait. No survivors were recovered from the *Pass of Melfort*, but three badly damaged bodies, all men, were found by people from Ucluelet. The wreckage, "much broken," according to reports, was found scattered over the rocks on the tip of the peninsula.

CHAPTER

14

The 1940s

WHILE THE SECOND WORLD WAR raged in Europe, North Africa and Asia, life went on much as normal on the west coast of Vancouver Island. The summers were often rainy, but generally beautiful. The winters, as always, were unpredictable. It snowed sometimes, and it rained often. Frequent storms blew in between November and March, usually without warning and often with devastating effect.

When the winds blew hard, they whipped the seas into raging elements of destruction. It wasn't only long-distance shipping that suffered from the storms. Local ships, boats and crews used to working the coast in all seasons also found themselves in deep trouble.

Varsity was a 67-foot-long American seiner (a fishing

boat) out of Gig Harbour, Washington. She was on her way home from a season of fishing off the California coast. On the night of February 5, 1940, while running off the Washington coast in thick fog, the captain saw a light flashing off to starboard. He assumed it was the Umatilla light and kept his course to pass Cape Flattery. Unfortunately, *Varsity* was well beyond Umatilla. The light seen was from the Swiftsure lightship, anchored over the Swiftsure Bank, 14 miles northwest of Cape Flattery and almost due south of Pachena Point.

To the surprise of Captain Joe Cloud and the crew, *Varsity* slammed into rocks east of Pachena Point about midnight. Another licensed captain, Herbert Ursich, was the mate on the seiner. He reported, "Some of the men were asleep and some were on watch when we hit." There was enough time to send out a distress signal before abandoning ship. Unfortunately, they gave incorrect information, telling would-be rescuers that they were on the Washington coast.

Ursich stated, "All seven of us got on deck and tried to launch the big lifeboat, but a big wave washed us all into the sea. All of us got hold of the upset lifeboat, but three of them slipped off pretty quick and we never saw them again."

As they closed with the shore, another wave knocked three of them off, leaving only one of the crew still clinging to the upturned lifeboat. The three in the water stumbled ashore and called to their shipmate. He answered that he would stay on the boat and hang on. His choice was the wrong one. He was never seen again.

On shore, the three survivors spent the first day huddled together at the base of a 60-foot cliff, hoping that by some miracle more of their friends would make their way to safety. They waited in vain. The stretch of beach they were on soon collected scraps of wreckage from the seiner. The three men cobbled together a ladder from driftwood and parts of the wreck. Using that rather precarious device, they worked their way barefoot, step by step, up the cliff. On top, after some searching, they found a trail that led to a linesman's cabin, from where they were able to send a message.

The American stations gave up their search for the missing boat on Washington's west coast and alerted Canadian authorities and the US Coast Guard. While a search continued on the sea for the other four men, the US Coast Guard cutter *Onondaga* crossed to the vicinity of Pachena Point. Her crew plucked the three men off the coast, out through the surf and onto the ship.

Another seiner, the 62-foot-long *Liberty,* was working a set in Barkley Sound and took a hefty blow on November 7, 1940. The weather was good that day, so the seven-man crew were pulling in their net close to shore. The engine was stopped, but the boat would not ordinarily have been in any danger. Then, a typical west-coast squall struck and lashed the sound into a sudden frenzy.

A crewman started the fishing boat's engine, but the propeller became fouled by a rope, leaving her without power. She drifted, much too quickly, toward a reef. An SOS went out, but *Liberty* was pushed ashore before anyone could respond. Two other boats in the area heard the distress call and raced to help. Taking risks with their own vessels, captains Gillespie, on *Gospak,* and Parson, on *Adriatic Star,* put them close enough to get lines aboard *Liberty,* hoping to pull her off. They were unsuccessful, the lines snapping under the strain. Before any other attempts could be made to free her, a comber swept under the two rescue vessels, picked up *Liberty* like a cork and smashed her onto the rocks, where she was broken up by later waves.

The crew, already in a life-threatening situation, found themselves wrenched from the boat and cast into the wild sea. Two men died that day. Another three came close to death when the storm carried them away from the rescue teams. They were fortunate to make it through the surf to shore and afterwards faced a long, hard walk to civilization.

The wartime blackout of 1943, in which lighthouses intended to guide ships along the British Columbia and Washington coasts were extinguished, probably had much to do with a Russian freighter steaming directly into Vancouver Island without any warning to the crew.

Uzbekistan was a 2,569-ton, French-built steamer with a crew of 50 men and women on board. She was well armed with big guns in order to protect herself at sea if necessary. On the night of April 1, 1943, she arrived off Juan de Fuca Strait en route from Portland, Oregon, to Seattle. She was working in the Pacific Northwest to collect cargo for Russia under the Lend-Lease program. After loading at Seattle, she was to have sailed for Vladivostok, on the east coast of Siberia.

Radar was still in the experimental stages, so it's improbable that *Uzbekistan* was so equipped. She would have been steaming more or less blind. That fateful night, there was only a light sea running, with no fog and no storms. Under excellent conditions, apart from the lack of coastal lights, *Uzbekistan* somehow ran full tilt onto a reef by the mouth of the Darling River near Pachena Point, scaring local Vancouver Island residents. But it was not the first time they had been frightened during the war.

On June 20, 1942, a Japanese submarine had managed to get close enough to Vancouver Island to fire up to 30 rounds of shells at the lighthouse at Estevan Point, just southeast of Nootka Sound. None of the shots hit the intended target, but considerable collateral damage was done when that action prompted the authorities to black out the lighthouses on Vancouver Island's west coast.

Soon after she hit, the Russian freighter announced to anyone within hearing that she was in trouble. For the coastal residents, coming as it did less than a year after the Japanese attack, the noise and bright lights from her distress flares and weaponry on board was a terrifying experience.

Appropriately, perhaps, the first vessel on the scene was the lighthouse tender *Estevan*. That little boat's captain called the Royal Canadian Navy to deal with the problem.

The navy sent a minesweeper to the location, but there was nothing the Canadian crew could do, apart from watch and listen.

At daylight, the Russians walked through the surf to shore without losing anyone and set off along the telegraph trail to Bamfield, where the minesweeper picked them up. *Uzbekistan* fell prey to the ocean's breaking waves and flooded. The next storm to hit the coast in that region rolled her over, and she was done for.

In addition to *Liberty* in late 1940, other small boats, such as tugs, met with unexpected trouble in similar ways and with equally tragic results. The wooden steam tug *St. Clair* encountered her final storm in a normally sheltered waterway on November 16, 1948.

St. Clair had helped a few ships and their crews get out of trouble. Three years before the storm that wrecked her, she discovered another tug's crew stranded on a log boom in winter after their boat went down north of Lund in the Strait of Georgia. She took them aboard and landed them safely.

Port San Juan is a long, wide inlet running northeast from close to the west entrance of Juan de Fuca Strait. It is fed on its northern corner by the Gordon River and by the San Juan River on its eastern side. Between the rivers are two First Nations reserves, and south of the San Juan River mouth is the small logging community of Port Renfrew.

Three known wrecks lie on the bottom of Port San Juan.

One of them is a tug. The other two—the brig *Cyrus* and the barque *Revere*—were additional hazards to shipping for 90 and 60 years respectively.

In December 1858, *Cyrus* was outbound for San Francisco from Port Townsend with a cargo of lumber. She had trouble with heavy weather in Juan de Fuca Strait and was trapped there for six days. Having taken a substantial beating, she took refuge from the storm in Port San Juan. While she was at anchor off the mouth of Gordon River, another storm struck. *Cyrus* ended up on shore, where the waves broke her apart. All of her crew survived.

Revere was no luckier. She was inbound from Honolulu to Port Townsend in ballast. Wind and currents worked together to take her off course and push her into Port San Juan. She went up on rocks at the entrance, in sight of the strait, in September 1883. Holed below the waterline and on her beam ends, she had to be abandoned to the sea. Again, there were no fatalities.

St. Clair steamed into Port San Juan towing a scow laden with fuel and oil. A fresh breeze was blowing directly up the inlet from the sea. It changed abruptly to a full gale from the southwest. In front of the logging camp, the swells became too high for the tug to attempt docking the scow. *St. Clair* struggled to move her tow out of harm's way but, as a result of being tossed around on the big waves, the tow line fouled her propeller.

Unable to manoeuvre and in increasingly large waves,

the crew hacked at the tow line with an axe, risking death on a deck that jumped and jerked and changed direction and slant every few seconds. By the time the line was severed, the tug had been tossed into shallow water and was too close to land. The wind is said to have reached "hurricane velocity" by then, and the seas just kept getting bigger and more arrogant.

Nine men, the full complement of the tug, fought for the survival of their little ship and for their own lives that day. Some tried to launch a lifeboat as the tug drew closer to breakers towering 20 feet high. They didn't make it. A wave bounced the tug off the seabed and bowled her over with her beam nearly horizontal. She came up again, but another wave swept the lifeboat and two men away into the surf.

People on shore at the logging camp watched helplessly as the valiant tug defended itself against the onslaught of the storm. All they could do was run into the surf, at great risk to their own lives, to assist the tug men fighting for their lives in the water. The tug lost its battle and turned over. Meanwhile, the battered scow had found its own way to shore. Of *St. Clair*'s crew, only six made it to safety. Three others drowned in the mountainous seas.

15

Vanlene's Simple Saga

ON JANUARY 9, 1972, THE Liberian-registered freighter *Dona Anita* was hit by an unusually strong storm off the west coast of Vancouver Island. She went down without a trace, taking all 42 persons aboard with her, including the captain's wife. Some time later, driven by the currents, a few of the bodies washed up far away at Ketchikan, Alaska.

Despite the area's reputation, the wild weather and dangerous waters on the southwestern coast of Vancouver Island are not always fully responsible for the fate of ships lost in the area. Sometimes ships meet a deadly end in the Graveyard at least partly due to sheer incompetence.

SS *Vanlene* was larger than most of the ships that ended their careers in the Graveyard. Registered in Panama, with a Chinese captain and a crew of 38, the 8,354-ton freighter loaded general cargo in Nagoya, Japan, in early 1972, bound for either a California port or Vancouver, depending on which report one reads. The greater part of her cargo was made up of 300 small cars, said to be Dodge Colts. If she was indeed scheduled for California, *Vanlene* had no business anywhere close to the dangers of the Pacific Northwest. A great circle route from Nagoya to San Francisco should have taken the 473-foot-long ship far to the south. Assuming, however, that she was en route to Vancouver, her course was remarkably close, considering her almost complete lack of navigational equipment.

Before leaving Japan, Captain Lo Chung Hung advised the ship's owners that "all our navigation aids had broken down." He also asked that everything be fixed before the ship sailed. The owners, so he claimed, chose otherwise.

Vanlene slipped her lines and turned away from Japan with almost no navigational equipment to guide her. Ahead was a voyage across nearly 5,000 miles of ocean. Outside Nagoya Harbour, the 29-year-old captain pointed the bow of his ship east toward the west coast of North America. His only artificial aids were two magnetic compasses, one gyro compass and four repeaters. The latter are used for steering, position finding and course recording. The ship's radar, radio direction finder, deep sea leader, taffrail log and mechanical log were not in working order.

Somehow, perhaps using inherited and instinctive

skills, Captain Lo found the coast he sought. It was unfortunate for him, though, and for his ship that a thick fog lay over the coastal waters and Vancouver Island on March 14, 1972. He had lookouts posted and presumably took depth soundings and listened for foghorns warning of nearby coastlines. As it turned out, none of that mattered. At slow speed, *Vanlene* found her way into Barkley Sound and passed a series of rocks that no one noticed only metres away. Then the lookout suddenly saw breakers to starboard and breakers to port. Before the engines could be run full astern, *Vanlene* slid smoothly up onto the rocks of Austin Island, where the SS *Tatjana* had struck 48 years before, also on a voyage from Japan.

Captain Lo thought he had hit the Washington coast, so when he sent out his distress call about half an hour after running aground, he gave a vague but completely incorrect location. In consequence, rescuers went looking for the distressed ship far from where she waited for their help. By this time, the surrounding waters had begun to play rough as a storm built up. The ship was listing well over to starboard with her bow on the rocks and her stern deep and awash. She had been holed and was taking on water at the bow and over the stern. By the time rescuers found out the ship's true position and arrived on the scene, the engine room had flooded. With no power, the pumps could not be manned to stem the inflow of water. A Vancouver-based tugboat, *Neva Straits*, sent a heaving line over to the freighter and was able to take the crew off, with some help from members of the Bamfield lifeboat station.

Although no deaths resulted from the final moments of *Vanlene's* strange voyage, considerable valuable cargo was lost, and the oil spillage (53,000 gallons of fuel) was catastrophic for the sensitive marine environment of Barkley Sound and its islands.

True to the tradition of the sea, which places the ultimate responsibility for a ship and its crew squarely on the shoulders of the master, Captain Lo graciously accepted the blame for the mishap and admitted that, in the final analysis, only he was at fault.

Vanlene clung to the rocks of Austin Island for a few years and survived countless storms. In the early days, many of the cars on board were retrieved, one at a time, by helicopter lift. While she sat there, when the weather allowed, local boaters ransacked her cabins and bridge for souvenirs. One day, when no one was watching, she slid stern-first into the deeps during yet another typical west-coast blow, her bow still aimed at the island that had claimed her in 1972.

Epilogue

TODAY MOST OF THE SHIPWRECK sites along the southwestern coast of Vancouver Island are well documented.
Amateur and professional divers have explored many of
them countless times, and local museums contain a rich
variety of artifacts taken from the sites.

Inevitably, time, powerful storms and the ever-moving
seas have conspired to tear the wrecks apart and bury their
remains under accumulations of silt. Marine growth also
obscures most of the debris, creating artificial reefs that
become new habitat for sea creatures. The Barkley Sound
wreck sites of HMCS *Thiepval*, *Vanlene* and *Nikka* are reasonably accessible and popular with knowledgeable divers.

Perhaps because of the increasing interest in shipwrecks,

the waters of British Columbia, particularly around Vancouver Island, have become a mecca for divers from all over the world. The province is often listed as one of the top dive sites in North America. Those same waters are, however, extremely dangerous to all but the most skilled of underwater explorers. Fortunately, there are accredited dive schools and escorted dive programs for the less accomplished.

Although new shipwrecks are rare in today's technological world, occasionally a ship will still go astray and find herself in peril. They are rarely lost, however, and deaths by shipwreck today are uncommon.

Bibliography

"Bark Janet Cowan Wrecked." *The New York Times*, January 13, 1896.

Belyk, Robert C. *Great Shipwrecks of the Pacific Coast*. New York: Wiley, 2001.

"Incidents of Soquel wreck." *Victoria Daily Colonist*, January 27, 1909, p. 10.

Mason, Adrienne. *West Coast Adventures*. Canmore, AB: Altitude Publishing Canada Ltd., 2003.

McClary, Daryl C., *The SS* Pacific *founders off Cape Flattery with a loss of 275 lives on November 4, 1875. The State of Washington, Washington Department of Archaeology and Historic Preservation*, 2009. http://www.historylink.org, file 8914.

McDowall, Duncan. "HMCS *Thiepval*, The Accidental Tourist… Destination." *Canadian Military History* 9, no. 2 (summer 2000): 69–78.

Neitzel, Michael C. *The Valencia Tragedy*. Victoria: Heritage House, 1995.

Rogers, Fred. *Shipwrecks of British Columbia*. Vancouver: J.J. Douglas, 1973.

_____. *More Shipwrecks of British Columbia*. Vancouver: Douglas & McIntyre, 1992.

Syme, Chuck. *The Wreck of the King David*. CD-ROM. Courtney, BC: Pickford Productions, 2008.

"27 Lost with Bark." *The New York Times*, December 29, 1905.

United States Commission on Valencia Disaster. *Wreck of the Steamer* Valencia: *Report to the President of the Federal Commission of Investigation*. Seattle: Washington Government Printing Office, 1906.

Wells, R.E. *The Loss of the Janet Cowan*. Sooke, BC: R.E. Wells, 1989.

Index

Acknowledgements

My thanks go to all those intrepid divers who have explored so many of the sunken shipwrecks in the Graveyard of the Pacific. Having experienced the underwater world a few times, I am in awe of your courage and tenacity.

Thanks also to the handful of nautical writers who have documented the stories of the people and ships that have braved the serrated coasts of western Vancouver Island. I am proud to stand among you.

Chuck Syme, a historical tour guide who specializes in the Gold River area of Vancouver Island, sent me his CD-ROM *The Wreck of King David,* which contains his excellent long poem about the ship's last day and the suffering of her sailors. Thanks so much, Chuck, I enjoyed listening to your tale immensely. Thanks also to the authors of so many websites dealing with the individual tales of shipwrecks in this region. You made my research so much easier.

My gratitude goes to Heritage House publisher Rodger Touchie, who asked me to write this book, and to managing editor Vivian Sinclair for putting up with me again. It is always a pleasure working with you two and your team. Finally, thanks to Lesley Reynolds, my editor for this book, for her careful work.

About the Author

Anthony Dalton is the author of eight non-fiction books, many of which are about the sea or about ships and boats. These include *Baychimo: Arctic Ghost Ship* and *Alone Against the Arctic*, both published by Heritage House. Anthony is the national president of the Canadian Authors Association and is currently working on another book about shipwrecks on the west coast, covering the distance between northern California and Alaska. He divides his time between homes on the mainland and in the Gulf Islands of British Columbia.

Also in the Amazing Stories Series

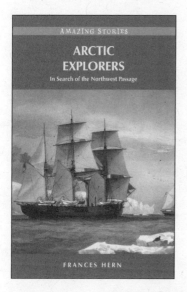

Arctic Explorers
In Search of the Northwest Passage

Frances Hern

(ISBN 978-1-926613-29-1)

The search for the Northwest Passage is a saga of hardship, tragedy and mystery. For over 400 years, the elusive, ice-choked Arctic waterway has been sought and travelled by daring men seeking profit and glory but often finding only a desperate struggle for survival. Spanning the centuries from Elizabethan privateer Martin Frobisher to RCMP officer Henry Larsen, the intrepid captain of the *St. Roch*, these stories of high adventure reveal why the Northwest Passage has gripped the imaginations of generations of explorers and lured them to its treacherous waters.

Visit www.heritagehouse.ca to see the entire list of books in this series.

More books by Anthony Dalton

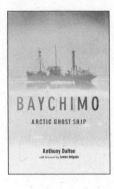

Baychimo
Arctic Ghost Ship
(ISBN 978-1-894974-14-1)

No vessel that sailed the Arctic seas has triggered imaginations as much as the legendary Hudson's Bay Company ship *Baychimo*. Dalton unveils the incredible tale of the hardy ship and brings to life the community of northern traders, hunters and sailors of which *Baychimo* was a part.

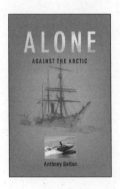

Alone Against the Arctic
(ISBN 978-1-894974-32-2)

Dalton's gripping description of his solo attempt to travel the Northwest Passage in a small open boat explores the irresistible lure of risk and challenge that continues to draw adventurers to the Arctic, a place like no other. Sidebars tell the story of another audacious Alaskan journey, a relief expedition in 1897–98.

www.heritagehouse.ca